Health Physics

A. K. McCormick and A. T. Elliott

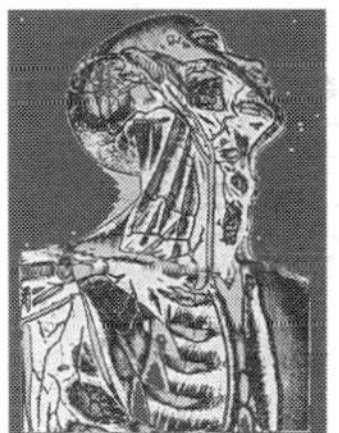

Series editor
Fred Webber

PUBLISHED BY THE PRESS SYNDICATE OF THE UNIVERSITY OF CAMBRIDGE
The Pitt Building, Trumpington Street, Cambridge CB2 1RP, United Kingdom

CAMBRIDGE UNIVERSITY PRESS
The Edinburgh Building, Cambridge CB2 2RU, United Kingdom
40 West 20th Street, New York, NY 10011-4211, USA
10 Stamford Road, Oakleigh, Melbourne 3166, Australia

First published 1996
Reprinted 1997

Printed in the United Kingdom at the University Press, Cambridge

A catalogue record for this book is available from the British Library

ISBN 0 521 42155 1 paperback

Designed and produced by Gecko Ltd, Bicester, Oxon

This book is one of a series produced to support individual modules within the Cambridge Modular Sciences scheme. Teachers should note that written examinations will be set on the content of each module as defined in the syllabus. This book is the authors' interpretation of the module.

Front cover photograph: Computer digitised dissection of upper torso and head anatomy.

Contents

1 Energy needs 1

Keeping going 1
BMR and temperature 3
Powerful stuff 4
Regulating body temperature 6
Other methods of heat loss 7
Reactions to heat loss 7
Preventing heat loss 8

2 The eye 10

Lenses, focal lengths and powers 12
Depth of field and accommodation 12
Common eye problems 14
Contact lenses 18
Perception of light intensity 19
Colour perception 20
Colour blindness 21
Social implications of colour perception 22

3 The ear 25

Structure of the ear 25
Range and sensitivity of hearing 28
Changes in intensity level 29
Hearing defects 30
Hearing aids 32

4 The production and detection of ionising radiation 34

The production of X-rays 34
Absorption of X-rays by matter 35
X-ray detection 37
Computed tomography 38
Gamma radiation in nuclear medicine 39
Scintillation detectors 40
Rectilinear scanners 41
The gamma camera 41

5 Medical imaging 44

Radiography 44
Ultrasound 45
Medical uses of ultrasound 47
Doppler ultrasonography 49
Nuclear medicine in diagnosis 50
Magnetic resonance imaging (MRI) 51
Light in diagnosis 54
Endoscopes 55

6 Medical treatment 57

Use of external X-ray sources in treating malignancies 57
External beam therapy 58
Surface and implant therapy 59
Radionuclide therapy 60
Ultrasound in therapy 61
Lasers 61
Photochemotherapy 64

7 Working with radiation 66

Radiation dose 66
Background radiation 67
Personal radiation monitoring 68

Answers to self-assessment questions 70
Index 73

Acknowledgements

3, Robert Tyrrell/Oxford Scientific Films; 6, Colorsport; 8*t*, Gordon Langsbury/Bruce Coleman Ltd; 8*b*, Duncan I. McEwan; 20*b*, Mark Fiennes/ Arcaid; 23*t*, Richard Bryant/Arcaid; 23*c*, Lucinda Lambton/Arcaid; 23*b*, photo by Victoria Hyde; 27, Biophoto Associates; 32, Roger G. Howard; 34, 37, 45*tl*, 58, 59*b*, Siemens; 38, 39, 41, 42, 44, 45*bl*, 48, 50, 51, 54, 59*t*, 60*tl*, 62, 63, Professor A T Elliott, Department of Clinical Physics and Bio-Engineering, University of Glasgow; 49, Dr M McNay; 60*tr*, Nucletron; cover, Custom Medical Stock Photos/Science Photo Library.

Every effort has been made to trace and acknowledge copyright but in some cases this has not been possible. Cambridge University Press would welcome any information that would redress this situation.

Energy needs

By the end of this chapter you should be able to:

1. understand that the human body dissipates heat energy all the time;
2. explain the meaning of the term basal metabolic rate (BMR);
3. understand that the daily energy requirements of a person will depend on sex, age, metabolic rate and any particular physical activities;
4. use data about daily energy needs with reference to the surface area and volume of the body;
5. estimate the power developed by the muscles;
6. describe experiments to measure the power output of leg and arm muscles;
7. explain why perspiration can increase the dissipation of heat energy from the body;
8. understand that under different environmental conditions the body can maintain its normal temperature through conduction, convection, radiation and evaporation;
9. describe how to prevent excessive power loss from the body through the use of insulating and reflective covers.

Keeping going

People need to take in food to give them energy. The body breaks down the food into the chemicals that are needed to generate energy: proteins are broken down to amino acids, carbohydrates to sugars and fats to glycerol and fatty acids. These chemicals are eventually oxidised in the cells using the oxygen from the air which has been breathed in. This is known as **aerobic combustion**. The most important oxidation reaction is of glucose, which releases about 17 MJ of energy from 1 kg of glucose.

Food materials are not used directly as an energy source in the body because the combustion processes are too slow to respond to sudden demands. Also the amount of energy released through these processes may be much greater than what is needed. So, the energy that is released in combustion is used to form phosphate bonds in a small molecule called **adenosine triphosphate (ATP)**. This can be transported in the blood to anywhere in the body that energy is required, and the energy released again by the breaking of the phosphate bonds. About 55% of the energy obtained from ATP is lost as heat in the conversion. The remaining amount is used to do internal work in the body or to enable muscles to contract and do work on an object outside the body.

The chemical reactions involved in aerobic combustion and the action of ATP are described in more detail in *Central Concepts in Biology* in this series.

Under extreme conditions such as heavy exercise, when oxygen is not available, the body can produce energy from the **anaerobic combustion** of glucose. The most important anaerobic pathway is the breakdown of glucose to lactic acid; this is very inefficient, producing only 800 kJ per kilogram of glucose.

Metabolism is the term for all the chemical processes that happen in the cells of the body. The amount of energy required per unit time to keep just the basic processes of the body going (such as breathing, heart beat, maintenance of body temperature) is called the **basal metabolic rate** or **BMR** (more correctly called the resting metabolic rate). It is equivalent to the power output of the body at rest and is measured in watts. The BMR varies from person to person and is related to age and sex *(figure 1.1)*. The following points are important.

- While both curves start at the same point, there is a higher average BMR for males than females of the same age. This is because females have a larger proportion of body fat which is mostly inactive in body processes.

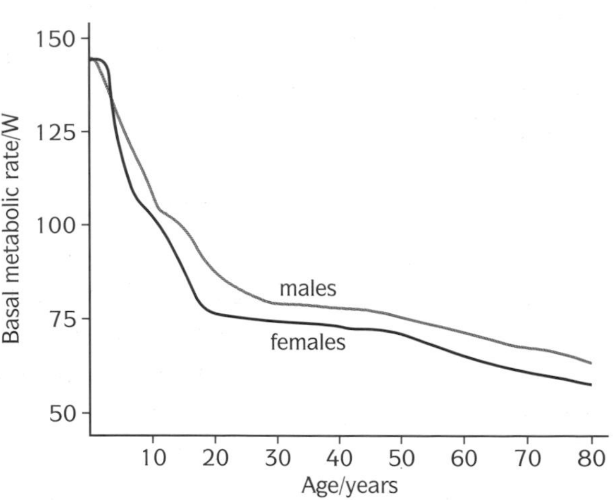

● ***Figure 1.1*** Variation of basal metabolic rate (BMR) with age.

- The BMR is highest in children because more energy is needed for growth processes. Also children have a larger surface area to volume ratio than adults, so they lose heat faster and need a higher BMR to keep the body temperature stable (see page 3).
- The BMR decreases with age as body size increases and the surface area to volume ratio decreases. Other factors may affect BMR as age increases, but these are not well understood.

BMR is almost directly proportional to the body's consumption of oxygen. When 1 dm^3 of oxygen is consumed in oxidation reactions, 20 kJ is produced. An average person requires about 10 MJ per day just to keep going. *Table 1.1* lists the energy content per unit mass and the energy equivalent of oxygen for carbohydrates, proteins and fats. The energy equivalent of oxygen, that is the ratio of the energy released compared to the oxygen consumed, is about the same for all foods, with an average of 20.2 kJ dm^{-3}.

Food	*Energy content per unit mass*/kJ g^{-1}	*Energy equivalent of oxygen*/kJ dm^{-3}
carbohydrate	17.2	21.1
protein	17.6	18.7
fat	38.9	19.8
ethanol	29.7	20.3

● ***Table 1.1***

Metabolic rate increases during any physical activity. Part of the energy is used in doing the physical activity and the rest supplies the increased internal energy demands of the body, such as increased rate of heart beat and breathing. The total metabolic rate for an activity is the BMR plus the metabolic rate required to fund the activity. For example, when digging a hole in the garden to plant a tree, the total metabolic rate might increase to eight times the basal rate. However, little mechanical work is being done by the body in this activity: the energy is being used by the muscles to change and maintain the position of the body.

Typical metabolic rates required for different activities are shown in *table 1.2*.

We can calculate the energy required for an activity as follows. In this example a 70 kg person cycles for 4 hours, and the metabolic rate for this activity is 7.6 W kg^{-1}.

$$\begin{aligned}\text{power generated} &= \text{mass of person} \times \text{metabolic rate}\\ &= 70\,\text{kg} \times 7.6\,\text{W}\,\text{kg}^{-1}\\ &= 532\,\text{W}\end{aligned}$$

$$\begin{aligned}\text{energy needed for this activity} &= \text{power} \times \text{time}\\ &= 532\,\text{W} \times 4 \times 3600\,\text{s}\\ &= 7.7 \times 10^{6}\,\text{J} = 7.7\,\text{MJ}\end{aligned}$$

If we assume that the average BMR is 10 MJ, we can calculate the increase in amount of energy required for this activity as a percentage of the BMR.

$$\begin{aligned}\text{energy needed as \%BMR} &= \frac{7.7}{10} \times 100\%\\ &= 77\%\end{aligned}$$

Activity	*Metabolic rate*/W
sleeping	75
sitting or resting	80–120
normal office activities	120–150
slow walking	150–450
jogging	300–550
walking upstairs rapidly	400–850
running	400–1400

● ***Table 1.2***

This means that in cycling for 4 hours this person would use up 77% of the entire energy that is normally needed in a whole day for the basic processes of the body.

In practice we use more energy than the BMR even if we are fairly inactive; typically about 13 MJ per day. In the example above, this alters the percentage increase in energy required to 59%.

Using *table 1.1*, we can calculate the mass of fat that would be required to fuel this activity. The energy equivalent of fat is $38.9\,\mathrm{kJ\,g^{-1}}$.

$$\text{mass of fat required} = \frac{\text{energy required for activity}}{\text{energy content per unit mass of fat}}$$

$$= \frac{7.7 \times 10^6\,\mathrm{J}}{38.9 \times 10^3\,\mathrm{J\,g^{-1}}}$$

$$= 198\,\mathrm{g}$$

This is the amount of fat that would be necessary to carry out the activity if it was the only source of energy for the body.

The efficiency of conversion of chemical energy in food into useful energy in the body is given as:

$$\text{efficiency} = \frac{\text{power output}}{\text{actual metabolic rate} - \text{BMR}}$$

SAQ 1.1

A person has a BMR of 60 W. Work is performed at a rate of 60 W with 25% efficiency. Calculate the person's actual metabolic rate.

BMR and temperature

All humans must maintain a constant body temperature of about 37 °C. This is because the chemical processes in the body are very dependent on temperature. A change of about 1 °C in body temperature changes the BMR by about 10%. So a person with a fever of 40 °C would have a BMR about 30% greater than normal. A drop of 3 °C in body temperature would produce a corresponding drop of about 30% in the BMR. Low body temperature can be useful for this reason. For example, animals that hibernate reduce their body temperature so that the food reserves of the body are used only slowly over winter. Human body temperature can also be lowered artificially during some kinds of major surgery, to reduce stress on the body during the operation.

Body volume and temperature

The rate at which the body produces energy is dependent on the volume of the tissue (V) while the rate of heat loss is more dependent on the surface area (A). A small body will have a large surface area to volume ratio, that is, A/V *(table 1.3)*.

This means that small people will lose heat energy at a faster rate than larger ones. This is particularly important for babies who need greater insulation when their surroundings are at low temperatures. In the animal kingdom, small homeothermic animals (which maintain a constant body temperature above the level of the air temperature by metabolism), such as mice and hummingbirds, must consume a greater proportion of food in comparison to their body weight than larger homeothermic animals *(figure 1.2)*. *Figure 1.3* shows the relationship between BMR and mass for different animals. The gradient of the

	Surface area A /m^2	Volume V /dm^3	Ratio of A/V /m^{-1}
small person	1.55	55	28.18
large person	1.98	80	24.75

● **Table 1.3**

● ***Figure 1.2*** A hummingbird sipping nectar.

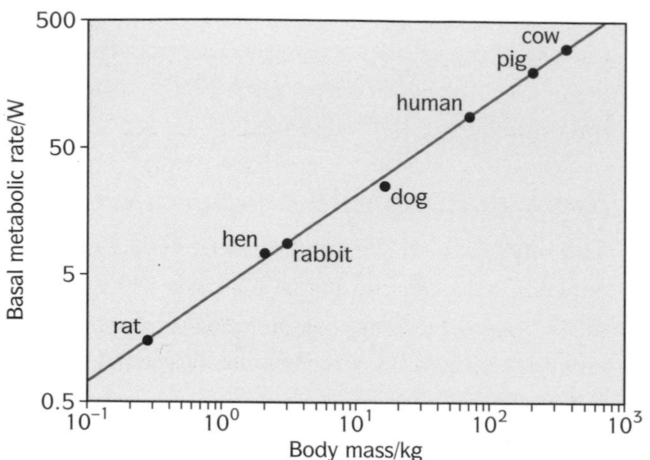

● ***Figure 1.3*** Relationship between BMR and body mass for different animals.

line indicates that the BMR is proportional to the $(\text{mass})^{0.75}$. Since mass is proportional to volume, this means that as animals become larger their BMR does not increase at the same rate as their volume. Assuming that surface area is proportional to $(\text{volume})^{0.67}$ (and therefore $(\text{mass})^{0.67}$), then BMR increases at a greater rate than surface area in comparison to volume. Note that the graph has a non-linear scale.

We can look at the relationship between heat loss and size more clearly in the following example of a large person and a small person. For the purposes

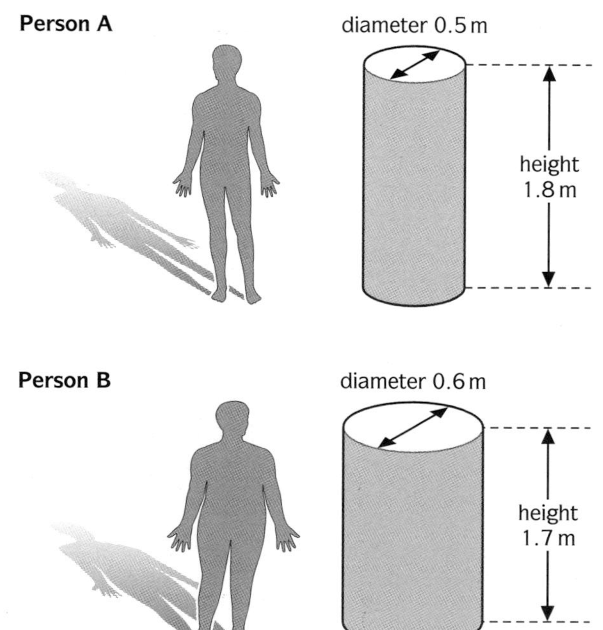

● ***Figure 1.4*** Representation of two people as cylinders.

of the calculation we can consider them as cylinders with the following dimensions *(figure 1.4)*:

person A diameter = 0.50 m; height = 1.8 m
person B diameter = 0.60 m; height = 1.7 m

By calculating the surface areas and the volumes, we can estimate which person will lose heat at a greater rate.

$$\text{Volume of a cylinder} = \pi r^2 h$$
$$\text{person A: volume} = 3.14 \times (0.25)^2 \times 1.8 = 0.35\,\text{m}^3$$
$$\text{person B: volume} = 3.14 \times (0.30)^2 \times 1.7 = 0.48\,\text{m}^3$$

$$\text{Surface area of a cylinder} = 2\pi r^2 + 2\pi r h$$
$$\text{person A: area} = 3.2\,\text{m}^2$$
$$\text{person B: area} = 3.8\,\text{m}^2$$

To calculate the comparison of heat loss the ratios of area to volume are:

$$\text{person A:}\quad \frac{A}{V} = \frac{3.2\,\text{m}^2}{0.35\,\text{m}^3} = 9.1\,\text{m}^{-1}$$

$$\text{person B:}\quad \frac{A}{V} = \frac{3.8\,\text{m}^2}{0.48\,\text{m}^3} = 7.9\,\text{m}^{-1}$$

Since the ratio is greater for A than B, the tall thin person will lose energy at a greater rate per cubic metre of body volume.

Powerful stuff

We have calculated the heat loss of the body, but what about the energy needed to carry out tasks, such as lifting or gardening? Any kind of activity increases the metabolic rate *(table 1.2)*, and it is useful to measure the muscle power needed for particular activities, so that we can compare the amounts of energy required for these activities.

It is possible to estimate the power of your arm muscles, for example by timing how long it takes to lift some bags up from the floor to a bench top. Remember that

$$\text{power} = \frac{\text{energy}}{\text{time}}$$

Assume that each bag has a weight of 80 N, the bench is 1.0 m from the floor, there are 20 bags and it takes 25 s to move all the bags from the floor to the bench top.

work done = force applied × distance moved × number of bags
= 80 N × 1.0 m × 20
= 1600 N m = 1600 J
time taken = 25 s

$$\text{therefore power} = \frac{1600\,\text{J}}{25\,\text{s}} = 64\,\text{W}$$

This is not just the power of the arms because other muscles in the body are used to support and move the body during the activity. So the total power developed by the body to do this activity has not been estimated.

To estimate the power of your leg muscles, you could time how long you take to run up a set of stairs. Typical results might be:

weight = 650 N
number of steps = 24
height of each step = 0.25 m
time taken to run up stairs = 6.0 s
work done = weight × height of step × number of steps
= 650 N × 0.25 m × 24
= 3900 J

$$\text{power required} = \frac{3900\,\text{J}}{6.0\,\text{s}} = 650\,\text{W}$$

A human cannot sustain this level of power for any length of time, and you might like to compare it with the power of a horse as estimated by James Watt, which he calculated as 746 W. James Watt was a mathematical instrument maker to the University of Glasgow in 1757–66. He is best known for his work that helped to develop and improve steam engines. The unit of power is named in honour of his work.

Task	*Efficiency/%*
cycling	20
swimming on surface	under 2
swimming under water	about 4
digging	about 3

● ***Table 1.4***

SAQ 1.2

A 50 kg woman runs up a flight of stairs in 3 s. The stairs have a height of 5 m.

a What is her power output in performing this task? (Assume she has a weight of 500 N.)

b Her BMR is $1.0\,\text{W kg}^{-1}$ and the efficiency of her muscles is 25%. Calculate her metabolic rate when going up the stairs.

c If the energy equivalent of oxygen is $21.4\,\text{kJ dm}^{-3}$, calculate the volume of oxygen used.

The rate at which work can be done depends on how long the activity takes. If you are young and very fit then you can produce up to $21\,\text{W kg}^{-1}$ but this can only be sustained for about 6 seconds. If you are taking part in a marathon race, you might have a maximum metabolic rate of $7\,\text{W kg}^{-1}$. A person whose job is doing physical work every day will normally produce less than $4\,\text{W kg}^{-1}$.

Studies have indicated that cycling is one of the most efficient activities. A championship cyclist approaches 20% with an external power production of 370 W and a metabolic rate of 1850 W. Typical efficiencies are given in *table 1.4*.

The maximum power output of the human body is variable. For short periods of time we can perform at very high levels but over a longer time we are more limited *(figure 1.5)*. It has been found

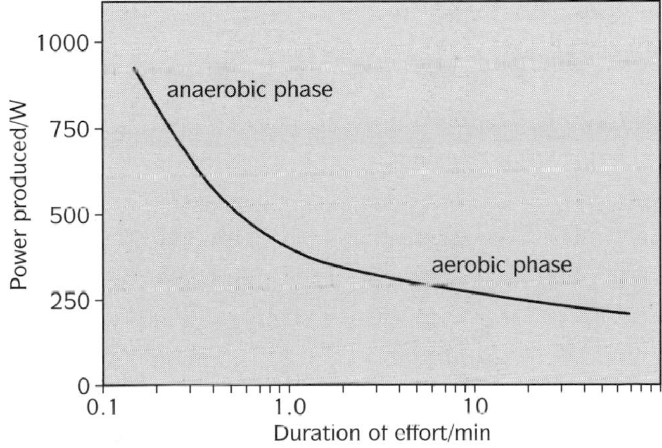

● ***Figure 1.5*** Typical output against time for cycling for an average healthy adult.

● ***Figure 1.6*** Carl Lewis.

that long-term power is proportional to the maximum rate of oxygen consumption in the working muscles. This consumption is typically $50\,cm^3\,kg^{-1}$ of body weight each minute. The power of the Olympic athlete Carl Lewis leaving the starting blocks in the 100 m has been estimated at 7000 W *(figure 1.6)*! Even this power is not all used to propel him forward since about 50% of the energy produced is converted to other forms of energy, such as heat.

Regulating body temperature

Human beings are homeothermic animals, maintaining a constant body temperature of approximately 37 °C irrespective of the temperature of their surroundings. This is essential because high body temperatures, called **hyperthermia** or hyperpyrexia, cause proteins in the cells of the body to start breaking down. At about 41 °C, this can lead to haemorrhaging (bleeding) in the tissue and brain damage can occur. At 44 °C death will occur in a few hours. **Hypothermia**, or low body temperature, causes damage by affecting the rate at which processes in the body can occur. At 30 °C, the temperature regulating system fails, heartbeat and breathing are affected and at about 27 °C death will occur.

The human body regulates its temperature by three methods of heat transfer namely conduction, convection and radiation. In addition, energy loss also occurs via evaporation, breathing and excretion. Over a 24 hour period, the average heat loss is:

from skin, by radiation and convection	73%
from skin, by evaporation of perspiration	14%
vaporisation of water in lungs	7.5%
warming air in lungs	3.5%
urine and faeces	2%

The levels of heat generation, transfer and loss must be balanced to maintain a constant body temperature.

Heat loss occurs mostly through the body surface by convection and radiation. The rate of heat flow from the organs to the skin can be adjusted by constricting or dilating blood vessels just below the skin. When they are dilated, heat loss can be five to six times greater than when they are constricted and blood flow to the skin is reduced. The hypothalamus, which is located in the brain, monitors and controls the blood temperature in the core (middle) of the body. It sends messages via nerves to dilate or constrict the blood vessels near the skin.

Heat loss can be increased by the evaporation of sweat from the skin (perspiration) and water from the lungs. When the core temperature inside the body begins to increase, the body starts dilating the blood vessels near the skin to increase blood flow in the skin. If this does not produce sufficient heat loss then messages from the hypothalamus cause the sweat glands to produce sweat. The specific latent heat of vaporisation of sweat (the heat energy needed to convert 1 kg of sweat from liquid to vapour) is $2.43 \times 10^6\,J\,kg^{-1}$ which is larger than the value for water ($2.25 \times 10^6\,J\,kg^{-1}$) because sweat includes sodium salts and urea. The rate of heat loss through the latent heat of evaporation rises rapidly, increasing between 10 and 20 times for an increase in temperature of 0.1 °C. Large amounts of heat can be lost this way since there is a large surface area and the body can produce a surprisingly large amount of sweat – up to 1.5 kg of sweat per hour. The production of sweat can be a very important cooling method.

SAQ 1.3

a Use the specific latent heat of vaporisation of sweat to calculate the amount of heat energy required to vaporise 1.5 kg of sweat.

b If a person produces this amount of sweat in one hour, how much energy is required per second?

c How does this compare with the power required to operate a 1 kW electric heater?

Other methods of heat loss

About 60% of the heat transferred from a naked body is radiated. This percentage is considerably reduced if the body is clothed. *Table 1.5* shows the main methods of heat loss.

If you are sitting in a classroom at about 23 °C then the rate at which you transfer heat to the surroundings will be about 170 W, provided you are normally clothed. Typical rates of heat loss by the different methods are shown in *table 1.6*.

These are typical values at 23 °C. They will vary with different amounts of clothing and at higher and lower temperatures. *Table 1.7* shows the rates of heat loss through the different methods at 33 °C and −10 °C, with clothing suitable for the conditions. In both cases the total rate of heat loss is 400 W but the relative contributions by each method to the total loss differ.

When the air temperature is high and a large proportion of the body is exposed, the main method of heat loss is by evaporation. At lower temperatures, when we wear additional clothes (and so the proportion of the body exposed is less), the main method of heat loss is conduction and convection.

Method of heat loss	*Factors affecting this loss*
conduction	size of temperature difference between body and surroundings, surface area of skin exposed
convection	size of temperature difference between body and surroundings, speed of air flow around body (this is low unless there are draughts)
radiation	absolute temperature (K = °C + 273), nature of the surface (rough/smooth, wet/dry etc.)
evaporation	size of temperature difference between body and surroundings, humidity (water vapour content of air), area of skin exposed
respiration	temperature, humidity

● *Table 1.5*

Method of heat loss	*Rate of heat loss/W*
radiation	35
conduction and convection	112
evaporation	17
respiration	6

● *Table 1.6*

Method of heat loss	*Rate of heat loss at air temperature of 33°C/W*	*Rate of heat loss at air temperature of −10°C/W*
radiation	32	32
conduction and convection	40	200
evaporation	320	8
respiration	8	160

● *Table 1.7*

Reactions to heat loss

If the core body temperature starts to fall below 37 °C, the hypothalamus releases hormones which stimulate the body tissues to increase the BMR and produce more heat. If this is not enough to raise body temperature, then the hypothalamus sends messages via nerves to the muscles to start shivering. This increased activity generates even more heat. The person might also respond to feeling cold by stamping their feet and rubbing their hands to increase activity of the muscles.

Animals with fur or feathers have another response to heat

● ***Figure 1.7*** Robin with feathers fluffed out.

loss. Tiny muscles in the skin react to low skin temperature by raising the hairs or feathers on the skin *(figure 1.7)*. This traps air next to the skin which acts as an insulating layer and reduces heat loss. In humans this is not very effective because we have little hair, and results in 'goosepimples' or 'goosebumps'.

Rate of heat loss can be excessive in very cold environments, or as a result of exposure or wind chill. (Wind chill is the cooling effect of wind speed beyond air temperature. For example, if the air on top of a mountain is blowing at $5\,\text{m}\,\text{s}^{-1}$ when the air temperature is $-10\,°\text{C}$, then the cooling effect on the body will be the same as if the actual temperature was $-19\,°\text{C}$.) If excessive heat loss is not prevented, and the body temperature drops to about 35.5 °C, the hypothalamus is affected and becomes less effective at stimulating the metabolic rate and other methods of heat production. At about 30 °C the hypothalamus ceases to regulate temperature completely, so that shivering stops and the blood flow returns to the skin, increasing heat loss. At this point rapid warming of the body by some external means is essential otherwise death will follow.

Preventing heat loss

When heat loss is excessive, the rate of loss must be reduced as quickly as possible. This is particularly important for sick, very young or elderly people who cannot move rapidly to create warmth. Rapid heat loss can also occur after vigorous exercise, such as athletes who can lose heat rapidly through perspiration. After a race this loss of heat will continue for some time and could reduce core body temperature to dangerous levels.

Heat loss can be reduced by the use of insulating materials. For example, covers on beds such as duvets contain trapped air. This acts as an insulator and helps to contain the heat that is in the body. Reflective blankets can be used in cases where heat is lost rapidly, such as the athletes mentioned above. The blankets reduce the rate of heat loss by reflecting the heat energy back towards the body *(figure 1.8)*. However, recent research indicates that these blankets may not be as effective as previous claims have stated.

SAQ 1.4

a Describe the different methods by which heat energy can be lost from the body.

b Which of these methods contributes the largest proportion of loss?

c Describe and explain a method of reducing this loss.

● ***Figure 1.8*** An athlete wrapped in a reflective blanket at the end of a race.

SUMMARY

- The human body gives out power continuously.
- BMR is the basal metabolic rate and is the rate of energy production needed for the basic chemical processes of the body.
- Daily energy needs for a person depend on age, sex, metabolic rate and physical activity.
- Daily energy needs are a function of the surface area and volume of the body.
- The average power produced by muscles is in the range 400–1000 W.
- Conduction, convection, radiation and evaporation are all important in maintaining body temperature.
- Rate of heat loss from a body can be increased by perspiration as a result of vaporisation of sweat.
- Heat loss from the body can be reduced by insulation, such as duvets and reflective blankets.

Questions

1 What are the main mechanisms of heat loss from the body and what affects these mechanisms?

2 The lift in an office has broken and you have to climb to the top floor which is 50 m above the ground.

   a What extra energy will you need if you have a mass of 75 kg and the muscles of your body are 15% efficient?

   b Discuss the factors that will affect both your efficiency and your BMR.

The eye

By the end of this chapter you should be able to:

1 explain how the human eye forms images of objects at different distances;

2 understand what is meant by *depth of focus* and *accommodation*;

3 describe and explain the differences between short sight, long sight and astigmatism;

4 describe and explain how these eye defects can be corrected by spectacle lenses and contact lenses;

5 distinguish between converging and diverging lenses and understand what is meant by the term *focal length*;

6 use the lens formula to calculate the focal length of the correcting lenses needed for long and short sight;

7 recall the connection between the focal length of a lens and its power in dioptres;

8 understand that the perception of the intensity of light and of colour is a complex process involving psychological and physiological processes;

9 understand that the perception of the intensity of light and of colour has social implications, for example, in architecture and in advertising.

Our eyes have several features which are remarkable even when compared with the most expensive cameras.

- We can observe events over a very wide angle while looking in detail at an object straight ahead.
- We have a rapid automatic focusing system and a built-in lens cleaner (blinking).
- Our eyes can operate over a large range of light intensities, from bright daylight to a very dark night (a ratio of 10^7 to 1).
- The cornea (see later) has a built-in scratch remover because it is made of living cells and can repair any local damage.
- There is a self-regulating pressure system which maintains the pressure inside each eye.
- The brain uses the images from both eyes to produce three-dimensional images.

The basic structure of the human eye is shown in *figure 2.1*. The key points are as follows.

- Light enters the eye at the **cornea** which has a refractive index of 1.336. In comparison to air, which has a refractive index of 1.000, this gives a large amount of refraction when light passes from the air through the cornea. In addition, the small radius of curvature of the cornea increases the refractive effect.
- The forward chamber of the eye is filled with **aqueous humour** which is a clear, watery solution containing minute amounts of salts. It has a refractive index of about 1.33.
- The **iris** is a circular, muscular diaphragm which controls the amount of light that enters the inner eye through the pupil (the hole in the centre of the iris). It is the coloured part of the eye.
- The **lens** is transparent and elastic, and is enclosed in a capsule. It is attached by suspensory ligaments to the circular ciliary muscles which can change

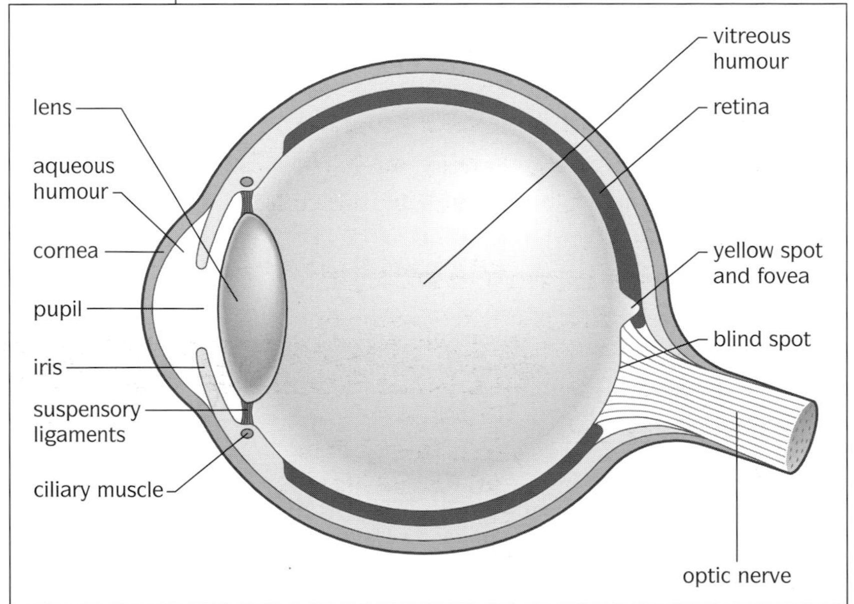

● ***Figure 2.1*** Section through the human eye.

the shape of the lens to make it thicker or thinner. Only a small amount of refraction takes place as light passes through the lens, though this can be varied depending on the thickness of the lens.

- The light then passes through the posterior chamber which is filled with a jelly-like substance called the **vitreous humour**. This maintains the spheroidal shape of the eye. Its refractive power, although slightly greater than that of the aqueous humour, is approximately equal to that of water.

  In the medical condition called glaucoma, the pressure in the posterior chamber increases, which alters the shape of the eye and interferes with the blood supply to the inner tissues of the eye.
- The **retina** is the layer on the surface at the back of the eye which contains the light-sensitive cells. These cells act as receptors for the optic nerve and change the light energy into electrical impulses. There are two types of light-sensitive cells. Around the periphery of the retina the receptors are mainly **rods**, which are sensitive to different intensities of light. Nearer the optical axis there is an increasing proportion of cells called **cones**. There are three types of cones each of which is sensitive to a different range of wavelengths corresponding approximately to the three colours red, green and blue. The full range of colours which we see is perceived by combining signals from these three types of cones. These signals are interpreted by the brain to produce the sensation of colour. There are over 10^8 of these receptor cells in the retina, with rods outnumbering cones by about 20:1. A comparison of the properties of rods and cones is shown in *table 2.1*.
- The **yellow spot** is an area of the retina about 1mm in diameter that is situated on the optical axis. At its centre is a tiny pit called the **fovea**. Here there is a high concentration of cone cells, and this is where we can see objects most clearly. In the centre of the fovea, where there are no rods, the density of cones is about 150 000 mm^{-2}. Here each cone is connected to a single nerve cell, to give even greater sensitivity whereas, elsewhere in the retina, two or more receptor cells may be connected to each nerve cell.
- All the nerve cells are gathered together into a bundle known as the **optic nerve** which transmits the signals to the brain. The **blind spot** is where the optic nerve leaves the eye, and is 'blind' because there are no light-sensitive cells at this point. The retinal artery and vein also pass into the eye at this point.

In the normal eye the rays of light from a distant object are refracted as they pass through the cornea and are focused on the retina. In these conditions some of the ciliary muscles are relaxed and so pull the suspensory ligaments outwards. These, in turn, pull on the edge of the lens, making it thinner (and of larger diameter) so that it has little effect on the light as it passes through.

If the object being viewed is close to the eye, the same ciliary muscles contract, reducing the tension that the suspensory ligaments exert on the lens so that the lens becomes thicker and of smaller diameter. This increases the refracting power of the lens so that the image of the object is focused on the retina.

SAQ 2.1

a Explain clearly the difference between the cornea and the lens of the eye.

b When you dive into water without a face mask objects are difficult to focus. With a face mask they are much easier. The refractive index of water is 1.33, of the cornea is 1.336 and of air is 1.00. Use these values to explain why this occurs.

	Rods	*Cones*
Responds	to dim light	to bright light
Wavelength at which maximum sensitivity occurs	500 nm (blue-green)	560 nm (green-yellow)
Spatial resolution	poor	good
Colour vision	none	needs at least two cone types
Rate of dark adaptation	slow	fast

● ***Table 2.1***

Lenses, focal lengths and powers

When parallel light enters a convex (converging) lens, it is brought to a focus at the **focal point**. The distance from the lens to the focal point is called the **focal length** *(figure 2.2a)*. For a diverging or concave lens the rays spread out after passing through the lens. The rays appear to diverge from a point which is behind the lens. This is called the focal point of a diverging lens. Again the focal length is the distance from the focal point to the lens *(figure 2.2b)*.

In the 'average' eye, the focal length of the cornea is 2.2 cm and of the eye lens is 5.5 cm. The combination of the two lenses gives a focal length of 1.6 cm (when lenses are combined their focal lengths are not simply added).

Opticians use a different measure, called the **power of a lens**. These powers can be added simply:

$$\text{power} = \frac{1}{\text{focal length in metres}}$$

and total power of two lenses combined = power of lens 1 + power of lens 2.

Power is measured in dioptres (symbol D). For example, an optician places a convex lens of focal length 20 cm in front of a patient's eye. The power of the lens can be calculated as follows.

$$\text{focal length} = 20\,\text{cm} = 0.2\,\text{m}$$

$$\text{power} = \frac{1}{\text{focal length in metres}} = \frac{1}{0.2} = +5\ \text{D}$$

Note that the SI equivalent of the dioptre is $(\text{metre})^{-1}$.

As the thickness of the lens increases, the focal length decreases and the power increases. The power of a convex lens is positive, and because a concave lens causes the light to diverge, the power of a concave lens is given as a negative value.

SAQ 2.2

A diverging lens has a power of −0.25 D. Calculate the focal length of this lens.

Depth of field and accommodation

Depth of field

In normal light, more detail is seen when we focus on a particular object because the light falls on the fovea. Objects both slightly further away from and a little closer to us than the one we wish to see are also in focus. The distance from the eye over which an object can move and still be in focus is

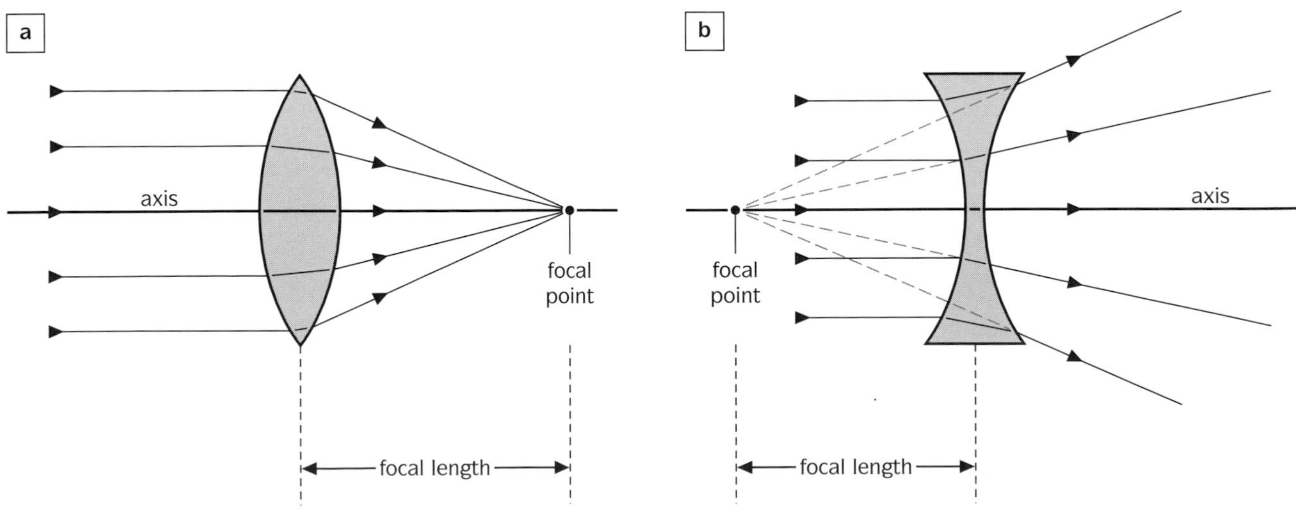

● ***Figure 2.2*** Focal point and focal length of **a** converging and **b** diverging lenses.

called the **depth of field** (x on *figure 2.3a*). The corresponding distance y behind the eye lens is called the **depth of focus.** It is large for distant objects because, if you move a distant object nearer to or further away from the eye, there is little change in the angles at which the rays of light from the object enter the eye. The angles of the rays of light from a near object are very different if the object is moved towards or away from the eye, so the depth of field for a near object is small *(figure 2.3b)*.

Accommodation

The lens of the eye is made up of layers of transparent fibrous material, which can be compared to the layers of an onion. The refractive index of the material is 1.413, which varies slightly from edge to centre. The front surface of the lens is almost spherical. The rear surface is not so regular since it bulges near the centre. The curvature of the lens varies with the tension which is produced by the surrounding ring of ciliary muscle. When the ciliary muscle ring contracts, its diameter decreases and the tension in the suspensory ligaments decreases. The elasticity of the lens pulls it back into a more spherical shape. When the ciliary muscle ring relaxes, its diameter increases and the tension in the suspensory ligaments increases. This pulls the lens into a flatter shape *(figure 2.4)*. The refractory power of the lens can change from about +30 to +20 D. This change in power is called the **accommodation** of the eye.

When the ciliary muscle ring is relaxed, and the lens is at its flattest and least powerful, then the eye is said to be **unaccommodated.** When the ciliary muscle ring is contracted, the eye has a greater power and is said to be **accommodated.** Note that the process of accommodation for near objects is an active one and can lead to fatigue, whereas the unaccommodated eye can rest on remote objects without fatigue.

If the power of the cornea is added to that of the lens, then total power of the eye can vary from +60 D (unaccommodated) to +70 D (accommodated). The ability of the eye to focus on objects at different distances depends on this ability to accommodate, that is to change the power of the lens. The overall distance from the lens to the retina does not alter. This is different to a camera where the power of the lens is fixed and the focusing is achieved by moving the lens towards or away from

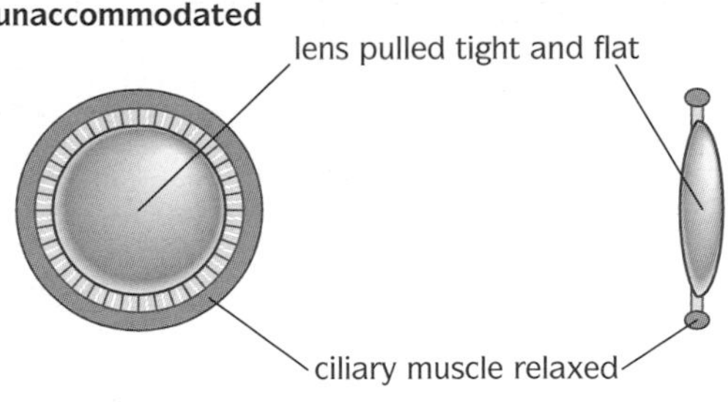

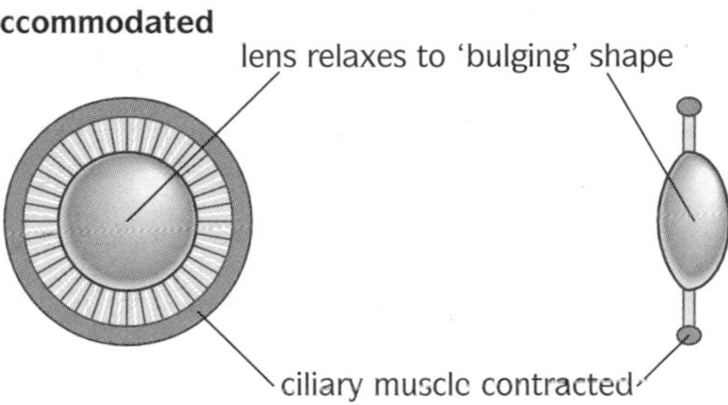

● ***Figure 2.4*** Changes in lens shape in the unaccommodated and accommodated eye.

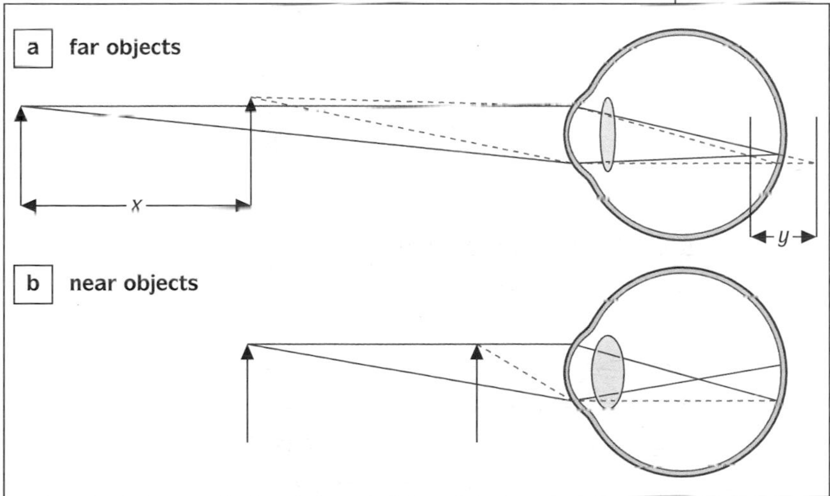

● ***Figure 2.3*** Focusing on far and near objects. In **a** both far objects can be focused on the retina at the same time. In **b**, although the objects are the same distance apart as in **a**, only one object can be focused on the retina at a time. In these diagrams, refraction occurs mainly at the cornea.

the film. A zoom lens also has a variable power to give variable magnification, but this is achieved by changing distances between the lenses, not by changing the shape of the lens in a fixed position.

In solving problems for this and other situations, we use the formula

$$\frac{1}{v} + \frac{1}{u} = \frac{1}{f}$$

where u = distance from the lens to the object,
v = distance from the lens to the image and
f = focal length of the lens.

Using this formula for the unaccommodated eye, when the power is at minimum (60 D) and we can assume that $u = \infty$, we can calculate the **lens–retina distance**:

$$\frac{1}{v} + \frac{1}{u} = \frac{1}{f}$$

$$\frac{1}{v} + \frac{1}{\infty} = 60$$

$$\frac{1}{v} + 0 = 60 \text{ (since } 1/\infty = 0)$$

$$v = \frac{1}{60}$$

$$= 0.017\,\text{m}$$

The lens–retina distance is often taken as 20 mm to simplify calculations.

Using the lens–retina distance, we can calculate the **near point**. This is the nearest object on which the eye can be focused when at maximum accommodation, that is at a power of 70 D:

$$\frac{1}{0.017} + \frac{1}{u} = 70$$

$$60 + \frac{1}{u} = 70$$

$$\frac{1}{u} = 70 - 60$$

$$= 10$$

$$u = 0.1\,\text{m}$$

Although the average eye can focus clearly on an object only 10 cm away, the eye muscles quickly tire at this degree of contraction. The nearest most people can read in comfort for a long time is usually about 25 cm, and this is when they are young and fit. If you try to focus on a nearer object using both eyes you will feel a strain caused by using the lateral muscles to make your eyes converge. This is more tiring than the effect on the ciliary muscles, so if we want to use close vision we usually close one eye.

Persistent eye strain that produce headaches can sometimes be due to weak eye muscles rather than refraction problems. This can be helped by simple strengthening exercises, like focusing both eyes on a pen as it is brought close to the nose or simply looking at the end of the nose.

There are no blood vessels in the lens so all the nutrients that reach the lens must diffuse in from surrounding tissue. As we become older, some cells in the centre of the lens become poorly nourished, die and turn white. The lens also becomes less flexible which reduces the ability to accommodate. Eventually the lens may become so opaque that little light is let through and the person becomes blind in that eye. This is known as a **cataract.** Cataracts can be removed by surgery but, without a lens, the eye cannot accommodate. So the lens is usually replaced with a plastic lens that is fitted inside the eye in place of the lens that has been removed.

The shape of the lens varies with age: in infancy it is almost spherical, in adulthood it is of medium convexity, and in old age it is considerably flattened. Young people have a much greater power of accommodation than adults and can read books held much closer to their eyes. As accommodation decreases with age, the near point recedes until, eventually, corrective lenses are usually required.

Common eye problems

Short sight (myopia)

When a person can see near objects (such as print on a book) clearly but distant objects appear blurred, they are said to be short sighted. It can be caused by several faults, such as the distance from the lens to the retina is too long, or the cornea or lens are too convex so that rays of light from distant objects are refracted too much. In each case the result is that in distant vision the image is formed in front of the retina so that light falling on the retina is unfocused again *(figure 2.5a)*. To correct myopia the power of the lens must be reduced, so a diverging or concave lens is used to bring points at infinity to a focus further from the lens and onto the retina *(figure 2.5b)*.

We can calculate the power of the lens required as follows. If for example, the **far point** (which is the greatest distance at which the eye can focus) is 0.2 m and the power of accommodation is 4 D, we can use the lens formula quoted earlier with the condition that v represents the distance in the eye from the lens to the focused image (which is taken as approximately 0.02 m). The focal length (f_1) of the eye can be found at the far point when $u = 0.2\,\text{m}$ and $v = 0.02\,\text{m}$.

a short-sighted (myopic) eye, uncorrected

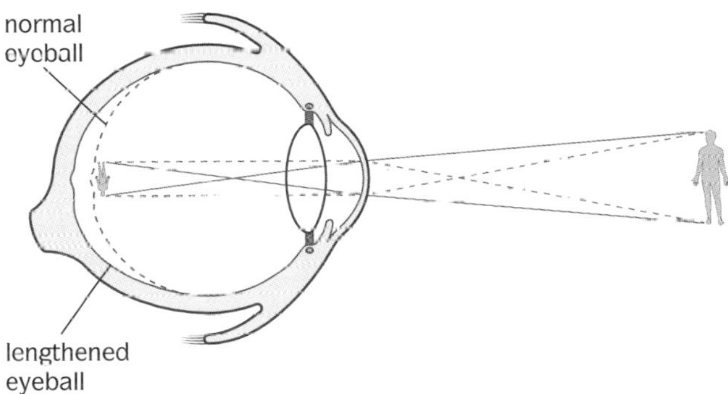

b short-sighted (myopic) eye, corrected

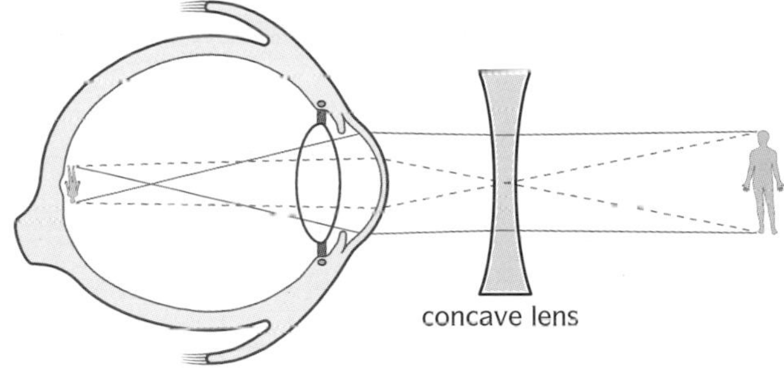

● ***Figure 2.5*** Short sight and how it is corrected with a concave lens.

This gives:

$$\frac{1}{0.02} + \frac{1}{0.2} = \frac{1}{f_1}$$

$$\text{So } \frac{1}{f_1} = 55\,\text{D}$$

We want the far point to be at infinity, so the power ($1/f_2$) of the combination of the lens in the eye and the corrective lens is given by:

$$\frac{1}{f_2} = \frac{1}{\infty} + \frac{1}{0.02}$$

$$\text{So } \frac{1}{f_2} = 50\,\text{D}$$

Therefore, the person will need a lens of power $(50 - 55)\,\text{D} = -5\,\text{D}$ to give a net power of 50 D when the eye is relaxed so they can see distant objects clearly.

SAQ 2.3

A myopic person has a far point of 1.0 m. Assume that the lens–retina distance is 2 cm. Calculate the power of the lens required to correct the short sight.

Long sight (hypermetropia)

When a person can see distant objects in focus but near objects (such as the type on this page) appear blurred, they are said to have long sight *(figure 2.6a)*. It is usually caused by a flattening of the lens or cornea or an eyeball which is too shallow.

As an object moves nearer to the eye lens, the eye must increase its power to keep the image on the retina. If the power of the cornea and lens is insufficient, as in hypermetropia, the image will appear blurred. The solution to the problem is to add a convex or converging lens of the correct power that will focus the light on the retina *(figure 2.6b)*.

Let us assume that a person has a near point (the shortest distance at which the eye can focus) at 1.0 m from their eye. For correct vision the near point should be 0.25 m. Using the formula quoted earlier, we can calculate the power of the lens that is required to correct the long sight.

In this case $u = 1.0\,\text{m}$ and $v = 0.02\,\text{m}$. We can

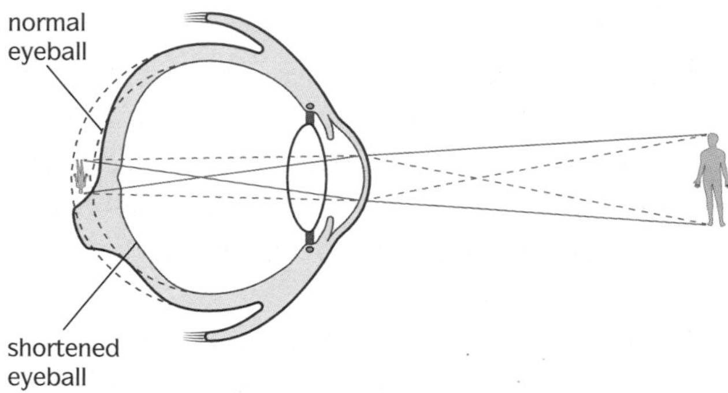

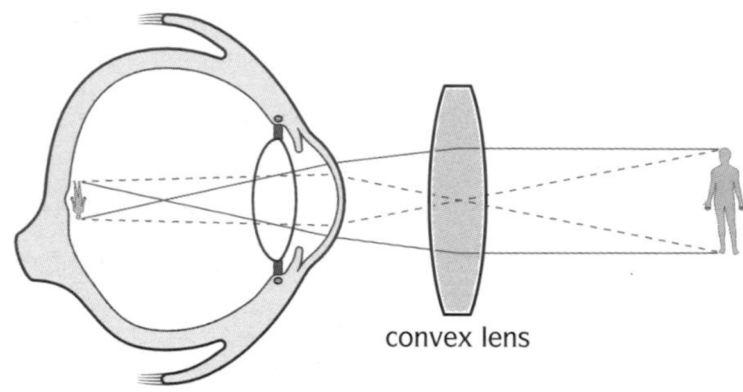

● ***Figure 2.6*** Long sight and how it is corrected with a convex lens.

calculate the power of the eye lens ($1/f_1$) with no correction as follows:

$$\frac{1}{v} + \frac{1}{u} = \frac{1}{f_1}$$

$$\frac{1}{1.0} + \frac{1}{0.02} = \frac{1}{f_1}$$

$$\frac{1}{f_1} = 51\,\text{D}$$

The lens power required to focus at the correct distance of 0.25 m is given as $1/f_2$:

$$\frac{1}{f_2} = \frac{1}{0.25} + \frac{1}{0.02}$$

$$\frac{1}{f_2} = 54\ \text{D}$$

The difference in powers is +3 D which is the power of the corrective lens required to bring the near point into the normal range, and to focus the image of a near object on the retina.

SAQ 2.4

a A person who is long-sighted has an accommodation of 3 D and a near point 2 m from their eyes. Calculate the power of the glasses needed to correct the near point to 0.25 m from their eyes.

b Where is the far point with these glasses?

Astigmatism

A person with astigmatism has difficulty in focusing the light entering the eye from different planes because the cornea is distorted. The position of focus varies depending on the angle at which the light enters the eye *(figure 2.7)*. A vertical beam of light may be focused on the retina whereas a horizontal one may be focused behind or in front of the retina. Light entering the eye from other angles will come to a focus between the two points. Astigmatism can be detected during an eyesight test by looking at a display of black lines radiating out like spokes from the centre of the field of view *(figure 2.8a)*. A person who suffers from astigmatism will perceive lines at some angles as darker and more sharply in focus than at other angles. This information can be used to determine the angle at which the axis of the lens must be positioned to correct the astigmatism. The defect is corrected using a lens with cylindrical curvature in the correct orientation *(figure 2.8b)*.

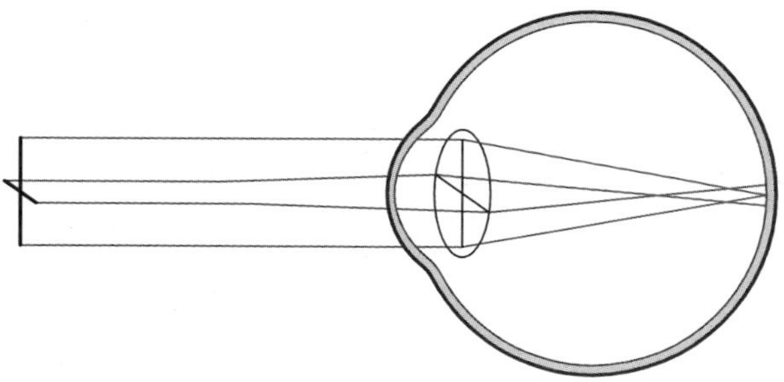

● ***Figure 2.7*** Astigmatism.

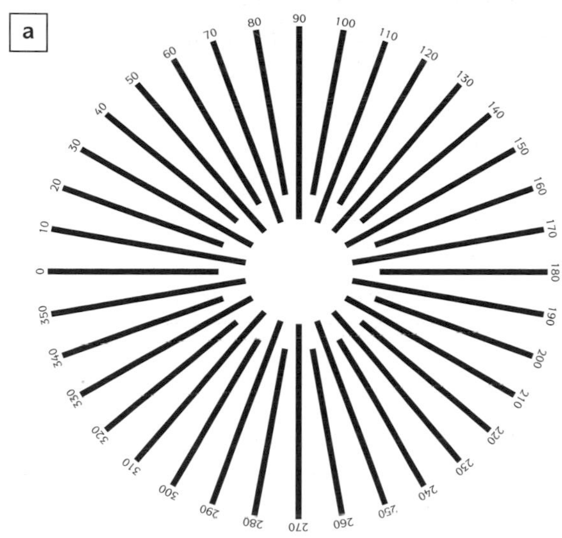

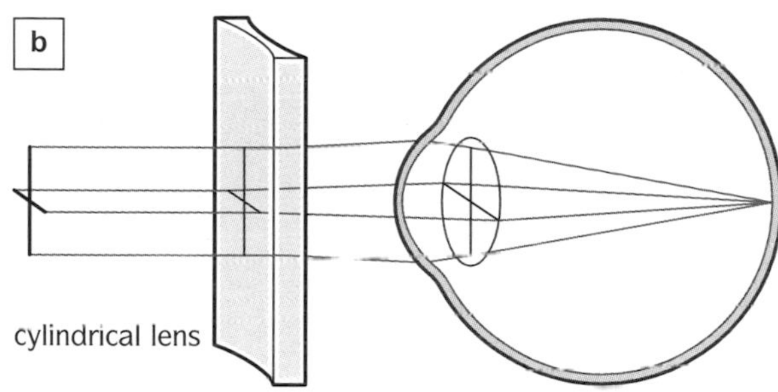

● ***Figure 2.8***

a A simple test for astigmatism. An eye with astigmatism sees lines going in one direction more clearly that lines in other directions.

b Correction of astigmatism using a cylindrical lens.

SAQ 2.5

a A person who wears glasses removes them and holds them some distance from the eyes. The glasses are rotated while looking at an object through the lens. The object appears to change shape. Explain why this indicates that the person has astigmatism.

b Why is a lens that is not symmetrical used to correct this defect ?

A typical prescription from an optician is shown in *figure 2.9*. This can be explained as follows for the right eye.

- The sph term indicates that a spherical lens is required. For distant vision the person is short-sighted and needs a diverging lens with a power of −1.1 D. The correction of +1.4 means that the person requires a converging lens to correct their near vision.
- The cyl values are to correct astigmatism, and the axis value indicates that the axis should be at 90° to the horizontal. The cyl means that a cylindrical lens is needed.

Similar terms apply to the left eye, and the prism value tells us that a prism is needed for both eyes to see in the same direction.

The normal eye test simply tests what is called **visual acuity**. The familiar chart of letters can be used to test vision. Perfect vision is called 6/6 or 20/20. This means that at 6 m you can read the line of type that a person with perfect vision can also read. (The 20/20 is the equivalent in feet.) If the result of your eye test is 6/12 then you can read at 6 m what a perfectly sighted person can read at 12 m.

Presbyopia or 'old sight'

Although many people are hypermetropic from childhood, even more become long-sighted as they grow older, and may need to hold a book at an increasing distance from their eyes to see the words clearly. Their eyes gradually lose their powers of accommodation, a condition known as **presbyopia**. Remember that accommodation is a 'flattening' of the lens as the tension at the edges is relaxed. This flattening is produced by the natural elasticity of the lens.

Right eye						Left eye				
Sph	Cyl	Axis	Prism	Base		Sph	Cyl	Axis	Prism	Base
–1.1	–0.8	90			Distance	–1.1			1Δ	
+1.4	–0.8	90			Near	+1.5				

● ***Figure 2.9*** Typical prescription for a person requiring bifocal lenses.

In young children the lens is very elastic, the power of accommodation is great and the child can focus on objects very close to the eye. Telling children not to hold books too close to their eyes is unimportant since they are making full use of their youthful abilities. At the age of eight we have an accommodation of about 14 D, but this drops to 3 D when we are in our forties *(figure 2.10)*. The solution is to provide corrective lenses for reading to increase the power of the unaccommodated eye. However, many people who develop presbyopia already suffer from other eye defects. For example, they may already have myopia, so now they will neither be able to see clearly at a distance nor close to. To correct for myopia they require a negative power of lens, and to correct for presbyopia they will need a positive power of lens. Distant objects are often in the centre, or above centre, of the field of vision while reading materials can be held below the centre. So, in such cases, **bifocal** glasses can be used in which the lens to correct for presbyopia is inserted as a segment in the lower part of the main lens which corrects for myopia. Corrective lenses can be made with more than two segments, or even a smooth gradation from positive to negative so that the distinctive line on the glasses is not visible. Such lenses are called **varifocal**.

The various defects are summarised in *table 2.2*.

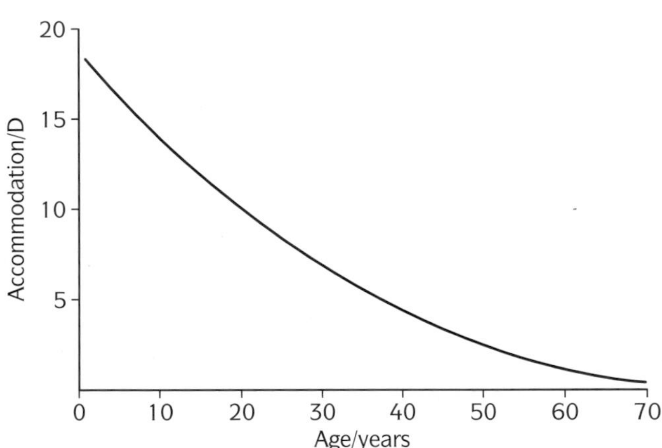

● ***Figure 2.10*** Loss of accommodation of eye with age. The decrease in accommodation usually becomes noticeable after the age of 40.

Contact lenses

The idea of lenses placed directly in contact with the eye is not new. Leonardo da Vinci suggested their use in the fifteenth century when he noticed that if he placed his face in a glass bowl of water with his eyes open his vision improved. It was not until this century, however, that the first contact lenses were made. Initially they were made of glass and covered most of the eye but modern lenses are made of plastic and cover the iris only.

Contact lenses can be used to correct eyesight defects in a similar way to spectacle lenses. They are placed in front of the cornea and are much smaller and thinner than spectacle lenses, being about 1 mm thick and 1 cm in diameter. They are held in place on the tear film (layer of fluid) of the eye by the force of surface tension. The reason that thinner lenses can be used is that the distance between the lens and cornea is reduced so that the lens effectively becomes part of the cornea. To correct for myopia you would need a weaker lens than in spectacles, but for hypermetropia a stronger lens is required. The curvatures of the surfaces of the contact lens are different, as the inner surface fits the shape of the cornea *(figure 2.11)*. Since the lens moves as the eye moves, aberrations or faults

Focusing problem	*Common name*	*Cause*	*Correction required*
myopia	short sight or near-sighted vision	long eyeball, excess curvature of cornea or lens	concave lens
hypermetropia	long sight or far-sighted vision	short eyeball, insufficient curvature of cornea	convex lens
astigmatism	–	uneven curvature of cornea	cylindrical lens
presbyopia	old age vision	lack of accommodation	bifocals if myopia also a problem

● ***Table 2.2***

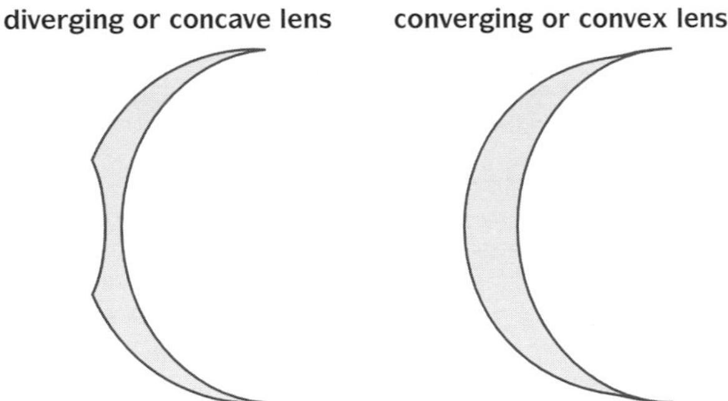

● ***Figure 2.11*** Cross-section of contact lenses.

which occur at the edge of an ordinary powerful glass spectacle lens are eliminated.

There are different types of lenses.

- Hard contact lenses are made of a tough plastic. They can be difficult to get used to wearing but will last a long time. Astigmatism can be corrected since the light enters the eye through a spherical surface.
- Gas-permeable lenses are made of a material which is rigid but will allow more oxygen to flow to the cornea.
- Soft contact lenses are made of a special plastic that allows a lot of oxygen to pass through to the cornea so that the lenses can be worn for a long period of time. These are shaped to the curvature of the cornea so they are more comfortable. Since the cornea may be irregular and these lenses do not maintain a spherical surface, they do not correct for astigmatism. These lenses are not very robust and are more expensive than the others. Since they sit on the eye they deteriorate more rapidly than the hard ones and suffer from a build-up of protein.

The latest contact lenses can be tinted to suit your moods and can now vary in external curvature like varifocal spectacle lenses.

Perception of light intensity

Rods contain the photosensitive pigment **rhodopsin** (sometimes called **visual purple**). Rhodopsin is broken down when illuminated and this action starts a nerve impulse in the nerve cell attached to the rod. Nerve impulses from the rods

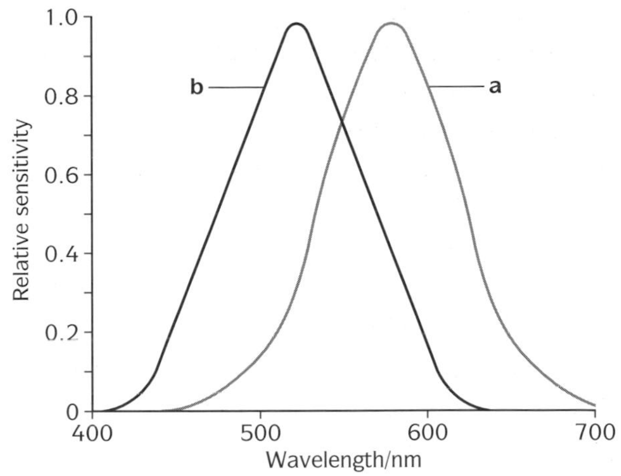

● ***Figure 2.12*** Relative sensitivity of **a** a light-adapted eye and **b** a dark-adapted eye.

travel along the optic nerve to the brain which interprets the signals as a pattern of brightness or light intensity. Rods react over a wide range of wavelengths *(figure 2.12)* and respond to much lower levels of light intensity than the cones. So in dim light we can detect the shape of objects but not their colour. This is known as **scotopic vision.**

The perception of light intensity is not related simply to the amount of light entering the eye. This is because the rods adapt to the prevailing light intensity. At high light levels the rhodopsin remains broken down so that the rod cannot respond to further stimulation by light. If the rod does not receive more light, such as in dim or dark conditions, then the rhodopsin can reform and the rod is ready again to respond to stimulation by light. This means that rods are more sensitive at low light levels. At high light levels, the cones respond to stimulation by light and the rods are not so important in the reception of light. This is known as **photopic vision**. The differences between photopic and scotopic vision are summarised in *table 2.3*.

The importance of the brain in the perception of brightness can be demonstrated using *figure 2.13*. This shows three identical grey circles which are viewed against backgrounds that reflect different amounts of light. Note that although all the grey circles reflect an equal amount of light, the brightness of each appears to be different because the

● ***Figure 2.13*** Effect of background on the perception of light intensity.

brain interprets them in relation to their surroundings. This helps the brain to distinguish shape and movement at low light levels.

The brain also interprets the perceived light intensity in other ways. For example, brighter objects are perceived to be lighter in weight or nearer than darker objects of the same size. This effect can be used to produce visual illusions in architecture, as shown in *figure 2.14*.

Scotopic vision	*Photopic vision*
uses rods	uses cones mainly
night vision	daytime vision
distinguishes only light and shadow	distinguishes colours
little detail seen	large amount of detail seen

● ***Table 2.3***

Colour perception

There is a complex relationship between our perception of colour and the perceived qualities of hue, brightness and saturation. **Hue** is what we call colour, and is determined by the wavelength of the light. It includes the seven basic colours of the spectrum together with others, such as crimson and purple which are formed by mixing violet and red from the opposite ends of the spectrum. **Brightness** is the subjective impression of intensity of light (the amount of light reaching the retina). **Saturation** is the purity of the depth of colour: when mixed with a neutral tone of white, grey or black, the colour becomes less saturated.

The cornea is opaque to wavelengths shorter than 300 nm, and the lens is opaque to wavelengths below 380 nm. An absolute long wavelength limit would be set by the absorption of light by the water in the cornea but the light-sensitive cells in the retina do not respond to wavelengths above 760 nm. The highest sensitivity (maximum response) of the eye occurs at 550 nm, which corresponds to green-yellow light.

Colour perception is made possible by the existence of three different types of cones. Each type has its own photosensitive pigment:

- blue-sensitive cones contain cyanolabe,
- green-sensitive cones contain chlorolabe,
- red-sensitive cones contain erythrolabe.

● ***Figure 2.14*** Use of light and shadow in architecture.

Each one absorbs light over a range of wavelengths, but the peaks are at 445 nm, 535 nm and 575 nm respectively. The absorption of light produces a chemical change in the pigment molecule, causing a small electrical potential to be developed which is transmitted by the nerve cells along the optic nerves to the brain. The pigment molecule is subsequently regenerated through another chemical reaction.

The sensitivity of the cones varies with wavelength as shown in *figure 2.15*. It can be seen that light of, say, 500 nm wavelength will excite all three types of cone, whereas light of 600 nm will excite only the red and green cones. The brain processes the relative strengths of the signals from the different kinds of cones to determine the colour of the object, like a colour television combines the three primary colours enabling the production of the full spectral range.

Every colour has a **complementary** colour which, when mixed with it in the correct proportion, will produce the perception of white; for example red + cyan (a blue-green colour) will produce white. Any colour can be matched using a combination of primary colours of specific intensities. Such colours as red, green and blue can be used in colour television and photography. Any perceived colour can be represented mathematically by a mixture of the three primaries *(figure 2.16)*. The three primaries define a triangle with white in the centre.

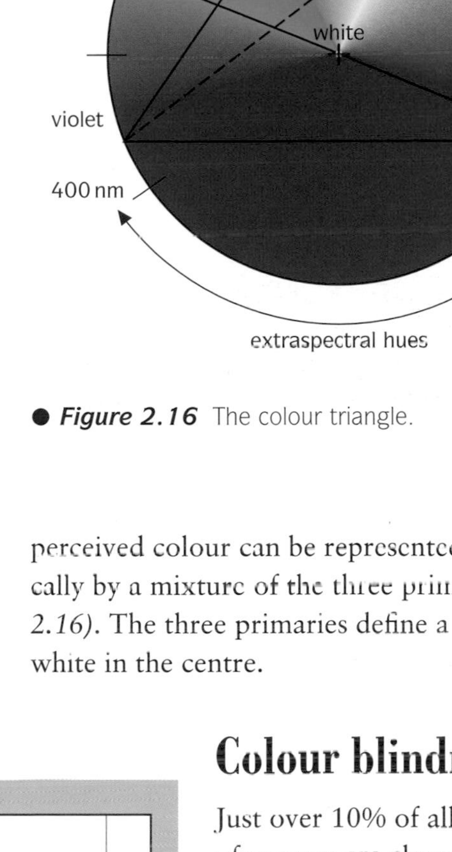

● ***Figure 2.16*** The colour triangle.

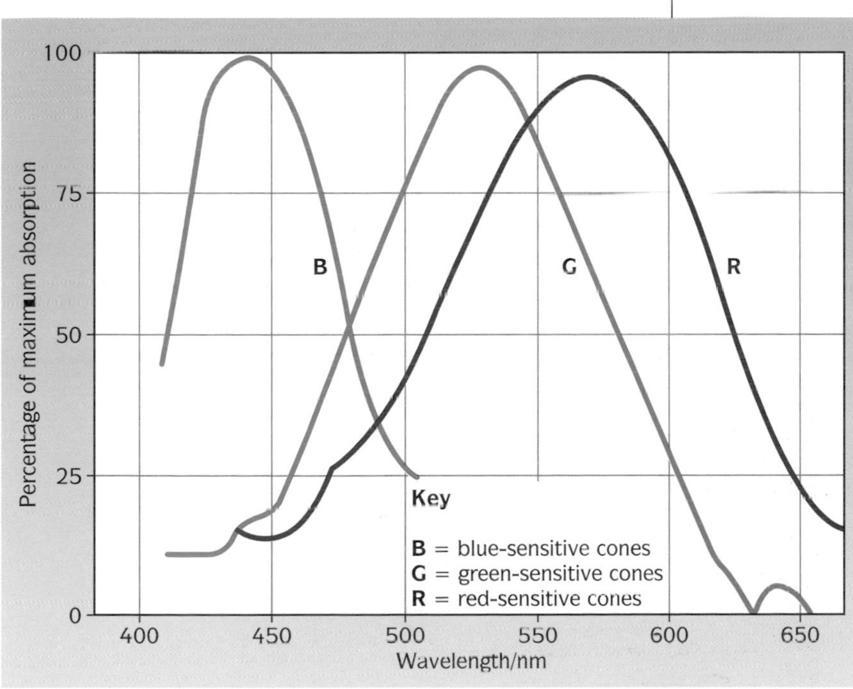

● ***Figure 2.15*** Ranges of sensitivity for the three different types of cones.

Colour blindness

Just over 10% of all men and 1.5% of women are classed as being colour blind. It is very rare for someone to be completely colour blind, that is see everything in shades of grey; most often they cannot distinguish between two colours. The most common type is red–green colour blindness which occurs in about 10% of men but is very rare in women. Tests of colour blindness depend on distinguishing between colours or whether a single colour is perceived where other people see different colours.

Colour blindness can result from a lack of one of the three cone types. However, most people who are colour blind do not have a complete absence of a colour system but have a reduced sensitivity to some colours. This is described as having **anomalous colour vision**. For example, in red–green colour blindness a person would need more red light or green light when trying to match a yellow colour than a person with normal colour vision. This can be tested by asking a person to view both a yellow light and a mixture of red and green light and adjusting the amounts of red and green until the two lights are perceived as being the same colour.

SAQ 2.6

What types of tasks or jobs might be affected by red–green colour blindness?

Social implications of colour perception

Colours clearly have a greater effect on us than just the perception of hue, saturation and brightness. They can affect our moods and reactions as the higher centres of our brain become involved in colour perception. The colours of red, orange and yellow are generally considered to give a warm feeling, whereas violet, blue and green are said to be cold colours.

Saturation of colour also plays a part in our reactions. For example, saturated colours of red and yellow 'feel' bright and busy. These are often used in fast food restaurants where a large number of people are needed to pass through in one day. Rather than telling people to leave, the effect of the colours is to make people feel that they should move on quickly after they have eaten. Saturated red and yellow, both in nature and in the fabricated world, are used as clear warning signs, such as wasps and ladybirds (which are unpalatable), fire engines and traffic signs.

The opposite effect can be given by using an unsaturated colour, particularly green or blue. For example, an air of calmness can be given to a waiting room of a doctor or a dentist where it might help to soothe the patient before treatment.

SAQ 2.7

Cathedrals and churches are often designed to give both an impression of space and of restfulness. How are colour and light intensity used in architecture to produce this effect?

SAQ 2.8

Look at the effects that can be obtained by using different saturations and hues of colours in interior decorating. How would you create a fresh, light atmosphere, such as in a bathroom or kitchen? What hues and saturations of colour would you use to give a warm, sumptuous feel for a lounge?

The use of different colours together can create a feeling of harmony or of discord. Look at the colour wheel in *figure 2.17*. Colours which are close to each other on the wheel, when used together, give a **harmonious** feel. Colours which are opposite each other give the greatest contrast. These are called **complementary colours** and give a bold effect. Colours which harmonise, emphasise features which are closely related. Colours which contrast can be used to emphasise differences or to make features stand out.

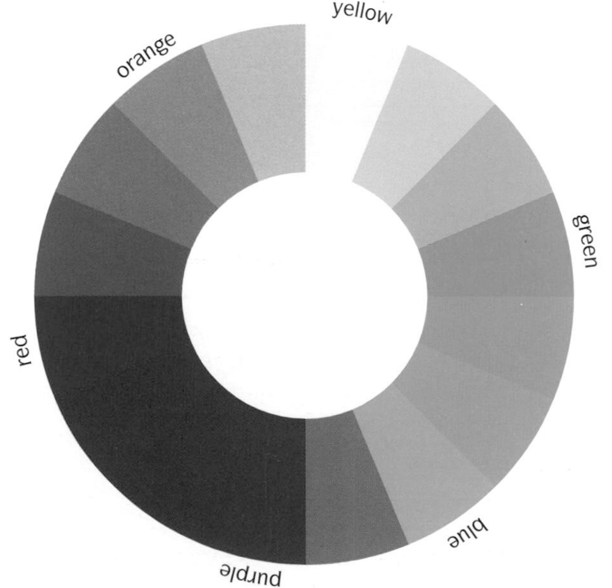

● ***Figure 2.17*** The colour wheel.

● ***Figure 2.18*** **a** and **b** Colour has been used in different ways to create an atmosphere in these two restaurants. **c** and **d** Colour is used in advertising to attract different groups.

SAQ 2.9

Look at a selection of colour adverts from magazines or on television. Try to discover a relationship between the colours used and the customers that the adverts are aimed at. For example, what colour combinations are used to attract young people to a product? Are complementary or harmonious colours used?

Colour, like brightness, can also be used to give the effect of weight or size, for example more saturated colours look heavier than paler ones.

SUMMARY

- The structure of the eye enables it to focus on objects which are at different distances from the eye.
- Depth of field is the distance over which a range of objects are in focus. Accommodation is the ability of the lens to change shape when focusing on objects at different distances from the eye.
- Short sight is when distant objects are blurred but near objects are in focus. Long sight is when near objects are blurred but distant ones are in focus. Astigmatism occurs when the curvature of the lens is uneven.

- Converging or convex lenses bring parallel rays of light to a focus on the principal axis of a lens at the focal point. Diverging or concave lenses make the rays of light diverge and appear to come from a focal point behind the lens.
- The distance from the lens to the focal point is called the focal length.
- Eye defects can be corrected using suitable lenses: concave lenses for short sight, convex lenses for long sight and cylindrical lenses for astigmatism.
- The lens formula can be used to calculate the focal lengths of any corrective lenses.
- The power of a lens in dioptres can be calculated from the equation

$$\text{power} = \frac{1}{\text{focal length in metres}}$$

- Colour blindness can result from a reduced sensitivity to some colours or from a complete malfunction of one of the three kinds of cones. The most common form is red–green colour blindness.
- The perception of light intensity and colour involves physiological responses, that is the reactions of the light-sensitive rods and cones, and psychological responses from the brain to the perceived colours and intensities. The psychological responses can be used, for example in architecture and advertising, to create visual illusions of distance, space, weight and mood.

Questions

1 A person is short-sighted and needs to have their vision corrected.
   a Describe what is meant by *short-sighted* and explain how it may be corrected. Detail any calculations that would be necessary for the correcting lens to be made.
   b What might happen to the person's vision with increasing age and how might this be corrected?

2 Describe the main features of the eye detailing the contribution of the lens and cornea in the perception of vision.

3 You are asked to design a rest area in a shopping centre. Describe any features of colour and architecture that you should take into account in your design.

4 a In the advertising and packaging of baby products, soft pastel colours are often used. What impression is being given and who is this aimed at?
   b What colours would you use when producing a baby's toy, such as a rattle, to stimulate the baby's interest?

The ear

By the end of this chapter you should be able to:

1 explain how the ear responds to an incoming sound wave;

2 understand the meaning of the terms *sensitivity* and *frequency response*;

3 recall the values of intensities for the threshold of hearing and when discomfort is experienced;

4 explain the logarithmic response of the ear to intensity;

5 recall and use the equation for intensity level in dB

$$\text{intensity level} = 10 \log \frac{(I)}{(I_0)}$$

6 explain that loudness is a subjective response of a person to a sound intensity.

Sound is a longitudinal pressure wave which moves through a medium by the oscillation of particles in the medium. The function of the ear is to amplify the small pressure changes and convert them into electrical signals which can be interpreted by the brain.

Structure of the ear

The structure of the ear enables a large range of frequencies to be detected and permits the listener to locate a specific sound.

The ear is shown in *figure 3.1* and can be divided into three parts:

- the **outer ear** collects and directs the sound into the auditory canal;
- the **middle ear** transfers the sound vibrations from the ear drum (tympanic membrane) to the oval window;
- the **inner ear** is concerned with the perception of sound and with balance.

The sense of hearing involves:

- the mechanical stimulation of the hair cells in the inner ear;
- reactions in the hair cells which produce electrical impulses that pass along the auditory nerves to the brain;
- the auditory cortex in the brain which decodes and interprets the signals from the auditory nerves.

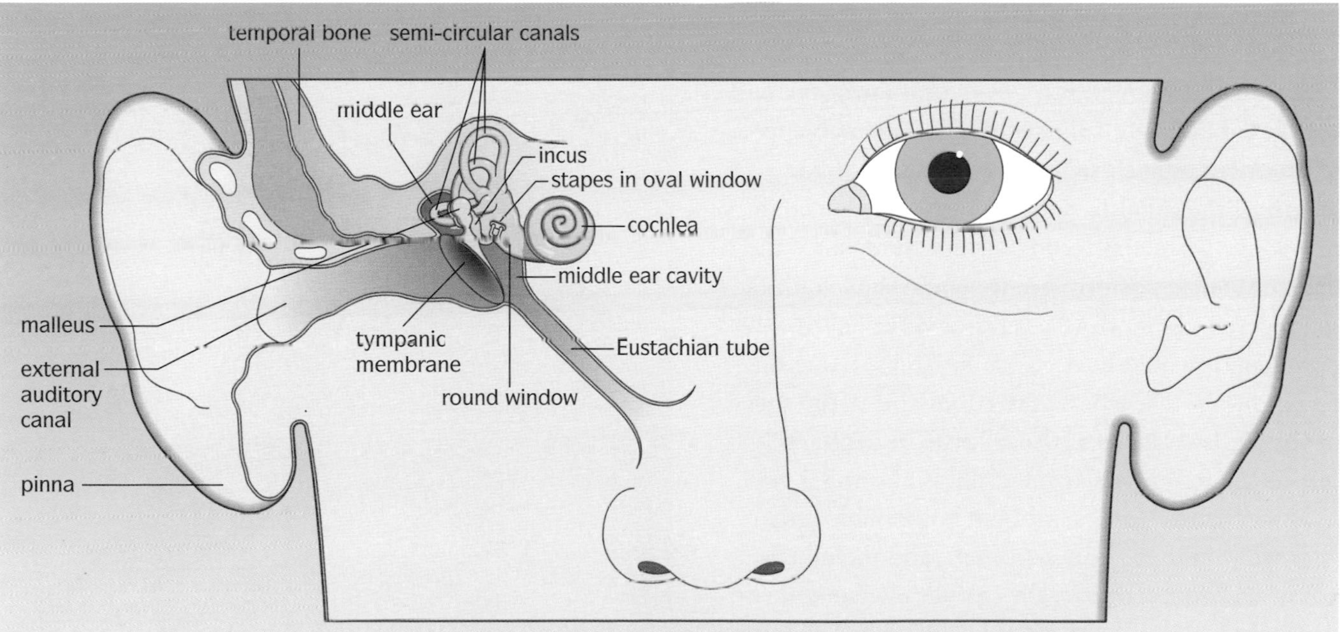

● ***Figure 3.1*** Section through the human ear.

Outer ear

The outer ear consists of the **pinna**, which collects the sounds and directs them along the auditory canal. The outer ear acts like an ear trumpet or horn, since the sound enters an opening of large cross-sectional area and travels along a tube of gradually decreasing cross-sectional area. At the end of the auditory canal is a diaphragm called the **ear drum** or **tympanic membrane**. This is a thin flexible layer of fibrous tissue covered externally by skin and internally with mucous membrane.

The gain or increase in pressure produced by the outer ear is quite large (approximately 20 times) at a frequency of 3 kHz. At the upper and lower ends of the speech frequency range the gain is much lower. A larger pinna would improve the gain for sounds coming from the forward direction. Cupping a hand behind the ear gives an effect similar to a larger pinna and is useful when the voice of a speaker seems to be just below the level of surrounding noise.

The improved gain at 3 kHz is, in part, due to the **resonance** of the auditory canal. Resonance occurs when waves are amplified by the structure they are in, simply because of the shape or construction of the structure. Resonance for a particular structure will only occur at a particular set of frequencies. The lower resonant frequency is the **fundamental**, which in the case of the auditory canal is 3 kHz.

Although the canal is quite a complex shape and the closed end is not rigid, there is a resemblance to an organ pipe closed at one end. Taking the length of the canal to be 2.5 cm, the fundamental resonance wavelength can be calculated, since the first resonance position occurs when the length of the pipe corresponds to a quarter wavelength. The wavelength would be $4 \times 2.5 = 10\,\text{cm}$. Using the equation $f = v/\lambda$, where λ is 10 cm and v, the speed of sound, is taken as $330\,\text{m}\,\text{s}^{-1}$, the fundamental resonance frequency of the canal is about 3.3 kHz.

Since the eardrum is not rigid but flexible (otherwise we would not hear anything), and the tube is not of uniform diameter, the calculation can only be approximate. However, it gives a calculated resonant frequency that is close to that found in practice.

Middle ear

The middle ear is an irregularly shaped, air-filled bony cavity which contains a set of three bones known as the **ossicles**. The bones are called the **malleus** (hammer), the **incus** (anvil) and the **stapes** (stirrup) *(figure 3.2)*.

The middle ear provides **acoustic matching** between the air-filled outer ear and the fluid-filled inner ear; that is there is a minimum loss in energy of the sound waves between the outer and inner ear.

The bones act as a lever system, amplifying the force received on the eardrum by a factor of about 1.3 times and applying it to the oval window. The area of the tympanic membrane is about $55\,\text{mm}^2$ while that of the oval window is about $3.2\,\text{mm}^2$. Since force = pressure × area, the two factors give a pressure increase of about 22 times.

The middle ear also contains two muscles which protect against excessively loud sounds which could cause damage to the hearing system. One muscle tightens the tympanic membrane and decreases the transmission of low frequency sound to the bones. The other pulls on the stapes and reduces the sound intensity reaching the inner ear. This change is not instantaneous and takes about 50 milliseconds, so that the ear is protected against sound changes which are gradual but not against

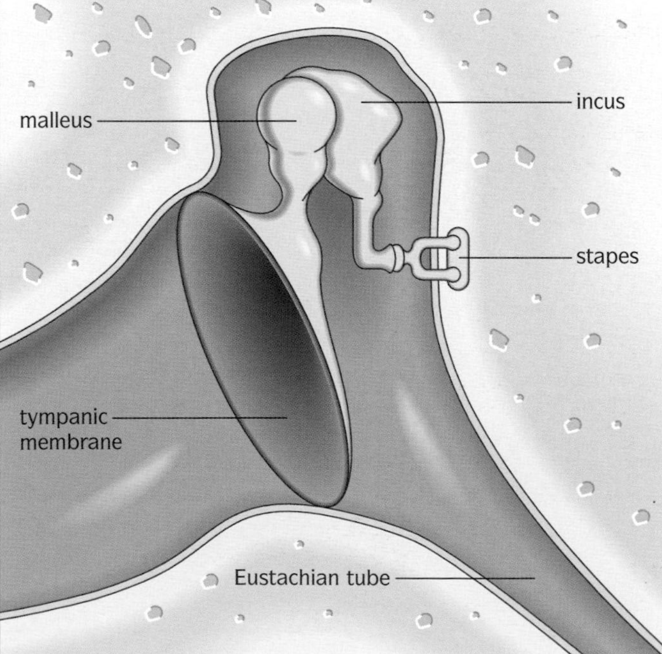

● ***Figure 3.2*** Section through the middle ear.

rapid changes such as explosions. These same muscles also protect our ears from our voices. The vibrations in the vocal tract are transmitted through the head to the ears and would sound extremely loud, except that the muscles are automatically activated before the sounds start and so protect you against the sound of your own voice.

The middle ear is connected to the back of the mouth by the Eustachian tube which equalises the pressure on both sides of the tympanic membrane. If the pressures are not equal, we experience discomfort. When the air pressure changes, for example when flying in an aircraft which is changing altitude, then swallowing (or chewing) causes the tube to open and the symptoms of the pressure change are relieved.

SAQ 3.1

When people are suffering from a cold they often experience discomfort in their ears when they are in an aircraft. Explain why this occurs and what they could do to help reduce the pain.

Inner ear

The inner ear is a fluid-filled cavity which contains the vestibule, the cochlea and the semicircular canals *(figure 3.3)*. The **vestibule** is a cavity lying between the oval window and the cochlea and connects with all the chambers. The **semicircular canals** are the sensors for the control of balance and are three liquid-filled tubes set at right-angles to each other. As the head is moved, the liquid in the tubes moves. Small hairs in the canals detect the movement and trigger nerve impulses which are sent to the brain where they initiate the reflex actions to maintain balance. Two small sacs at the base of the semicircular canals register the position of the head relative to the upright position so that a change in angle, or an upside-down position, can be detected.

The **cochlea** is so called because it is shaped like a coche or snail's shell. It is a three-chambered tube which is filled with fluid and twisted into a spiral of approximately $2\frac{3}{4}$ turns. The diameter of the tube decreases from the base to the apex *(figure 3.3)*. Two of the chambers, the **vestibular** and **tympanic** chambers, are joined together at the apex of the spiral and are filled with a clear fluid called **perilymph.** The base of the vestibular chamber connects with the **oval window** and the base of the tympanic chamber connects to the **round window.** Between these two chambers is the **cochlear duct,** which is filled with a fluid known as **endolymph.**

The **basilar membrane** separates the cochlear duct from the tympanic chamber and supports a single layer of sensory hair cells on its inner surface *(figure 3.4)*. These hair cells project across the endolymph-filled duct to the **tectorial membrane,**

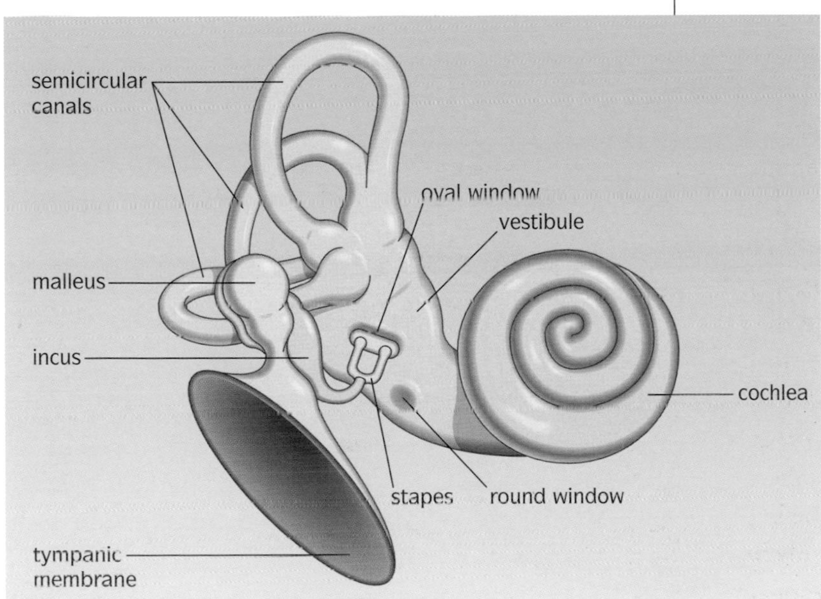

● ***Figure 3.3*** Section through the inner ear.

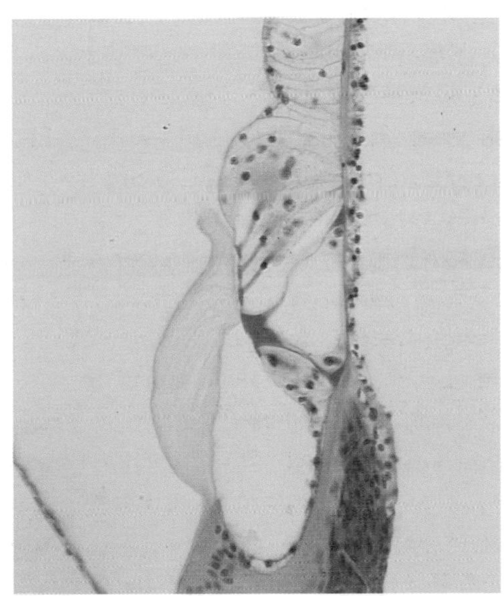

● ***Figure 3.4*** Electron micrograph of hair cells in the organ of Corti.

which is part of the wall between the cochlear duct and the vestibular chamber. This structure is known as the **organ of Corti** (see *figure 3.5*).

The increase in pressure produced by the action of the middle ear is necessary to produce vibrations, as a longitudinal wave, in the perilymph (remember that liquids have a greater inertia than air). The waves which travel along the perilymph in the vestibular and tympanic chambers are transmitted to the endolymph in the cochlear duct. These vibrations cause the hair cells to move and send signals along the auditory nerve to the brain. Exactly how the cochlea works is not well understood, but the higher frequencies excite the cells nearest to the base and lower frequencies are transmitted further to excite the cells nearest to the apex of the cochlea. The brain decodes the signals from each area of hair cells to determine the frequencies present and distinguish the sounds received by the ear.

Increasing loudness is detected in several ways:

- firstly, by an increase in the amplitude of the signal generated by each hair cell;
- secondly, as a greater proportion of the hair cells in the appropriate area are stimulated;
- thirdly, as hair cells in adjacent areas are stimulated.

Since the cochlea lies within the bone of the skull, it is possible to excite the cochlear fluid by causing vibrations in the bone itself. This can be accomplished by, for example, placing a tuning fork against any projection of the skull, particularly the mastoid process. Sound will be heard corresponding to the frequency at which the fork is vibrating. When underwater, most of the sound received by the cochlea has been transmitted through the skull.

Range and sensitivity of hearing

The normal frequency range of hearing is from 20 to 20 000 Hz (20 kHz) for adults. In younger children, the upper end of the range may be as high as 30 kHz but this decreases with age.

The human ear can distinguish a remarkably small change in frequency, of about 0.1%. This can be compared with the a musical semi-tone which has a frequency change of about 6% (a full tone would be from doh to ray in the musical scale). Between 60 and 1000 Hz we can distinguish differences of 2–3 Hz. Beyond 1000 Hz it is more difficult to distinguish between frequencies that are close together.

Sound intensity is a measure of the power of the sound over a unit of area. The smallest sound intensity which can be heard at a given frequency is called the **threshold of hearing**. This is shown as a function of frequency in *figure 3.6*, where frequency is plotted on a logarithmic scale. A logarithmic scale is used because of the very large range of frequencies involved which would be difficult to plot on a linear scale. The graph shows that the human ear is most sensitive at about 2 kHz.

At low sound intensities very small changes in the intensity can be perceived, but at high intensities the same change may not be noticed. This is because equal changes in intensity are not perceived as equal changes in loudness. The relationship between intensity and intensity level is a logarithmic one.

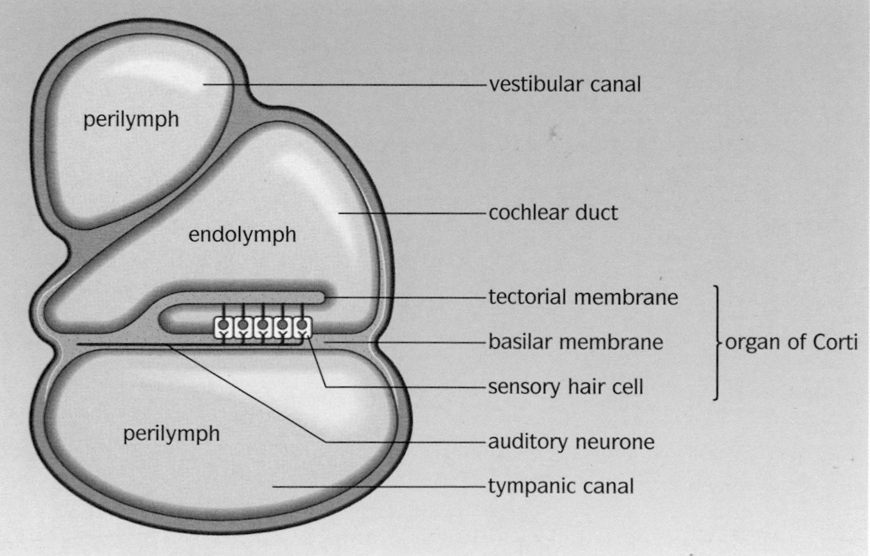

● ***Figure 3.5*** Section through the organ of Corti.

The decibel

To define an intensity level we need a base level against which other intensities can be measured. At about 1000 Hz the lowest intensity of sound that anyone can hear is $10^{-12}\,\mathrm{W\,m^{-2}}$. This is chosen as the threshold intensity (I_0) and the intensity level of a sound of intensity I in bels (named after Alexander Graham Bell who invented the telephone and was a teacher of the deaf) is defined as

$$\text{intensity level} = \log \frac{I}{I_0}\,\mathrm{B}$$

Since the bel is a large unit the standard unit of intensity level is the decibel (dB), which is defined as 1 B = 10 dB. So the equation becomes

$$\text{intensity level} = 10 \log \frac{I}{I_0}\,\mathrm{dB}$$

For example, a sound has an intensity of $10^{-7}\,\mathrm{Wm^{-2}}$, so the intensity level in decibels is

$$10 \log_{10} \frac{10^{-7}}{10^{-12}} = 10 \log_{10} (10^5) = 50\,\mathrm{dB}$$

SAQ 3.2

When new windows are put into a house, the intensity of the sounds measured in a room changes from $10^{-4}\,\mathrm{Wm^{-2}}$ before to $10^{-8}\,\mathrm{Wm^{-2}}$ after installation. Calculate the change in intensity levels in decibels.

Changes in intensity level

The relationship between sound intensity and intensity level is a logarithmic one. So if the intensity is doubled then the intensity level is increased by about 3 dB, as shown in the following example.

Two television sets are showing different programmes; the intensity level of the sound at a distance of 2 m from each set has an average of 50 dB. What is the average intensity level when both sets are switched on?

$$\text{intensity level for one set} = 50\,\mathrm{dB} = 10 \log \frac{I}{I_0}$$

When both sets are on the total intensity will be $I + I = 2I$.

$$\text{So the intensity level for two sets} = 10 \log \frac{2I}{I_0}$$

$$= 10 \log 2 + 10 \log \frac{I}{I_0}$$

$$= 10 \log 2 + \text{intensity level for one set}$$

$$= 3 + 50\,\mathrm{dB}$$

$$= 53\,\mathrm{dB}$$

The difference in intensity levels between two sounds of intensities I_1 and I_2 can be calculated by subtraction:

$$10 \left\{\log_{10} \left(\frac{I_2}{I_0}\right) - \log_{10} \left(\frac{I_1}{I_0}\right)\right\}$$

which becomes

$$10 \log_{10} \left(\frac{I_2}{I_1}\right)$$

Typical noise levels are given in *table 3.1*. At 100–110 dB conversation becomes impossible.

The human ear can respond to intensities of sound ranging from as low as $10^{-12}\,\mathrm{W\,m^{-2}}$ to as high as $1\,\mathrm{W\,m^{-2}}$. Measurements of our hearing response are subjective but there are three thresholds. The **threshold of hearing** is the minimum intensity that is just audible at a given frequency. The **threshold of feeling** occurs at high intensity

Noise level/dB	*Situation*
0	minimum sound that can be heard
10	movement of leaves in trees
20	quiet lane
30	whispering
40	quiet conversation
50	noise in the average home
60	normal conversation at 1 m
70	inside a large shop
80	about 18 m from a busy motorway (the first danger level)
90	inside a heavy truck or underground train
100	lorry at a distance of 8 m in a narrow street
110	pop group at 1 m or train whistle at 15 m
120	aircraft at 175 m
130	jet engine at 35 m

● *Table 3.1*

(approximately 120 dB) and is characterised by a tickling sensation in the ear which occurs when the ossicles vibrate so strongly that they strike the wall of the middle ear. The normal hearing range lies between these two limits *(figure 3.6)*. At about 140 dB, there is a **pain threshold**, and beyond 160 dB the tympanic membrane may rupture.

Loudness and intensity level

Loudness and intensity level are not the same quantities. The intensity level has a distinct meaning since it is defined in comparison to a threshold of hearing at which no sound is detected by the ear. Loudness depends both on the intensity and on the hearing capability of the observer and is obviously subjective. To overcome this problem, quantitative methods have been developed.

In one method, all sounds are compared with the absolute intensity of sound of frequency 1000 Hz. The intensity of the 1000 Hz sound is adjusted until it is perceived as being as loud as the source being measured. If the intensity of the 1000 Hz sound at this point is 50 dB, then the second source is said to be 50 dB also. This method, known as **phon measurement**, is not easy to carry out in many practical situations.

This led to the development of several 'weighted' scales of measurement, the A-scale being adopted almost universally; it is denoted dB(A) or, more commonly, dBA. In this scale, a set of weightings is applied to the intensities at different frequencies so that the scale has a response similar to that of the human ear *(figure 3.7)*.

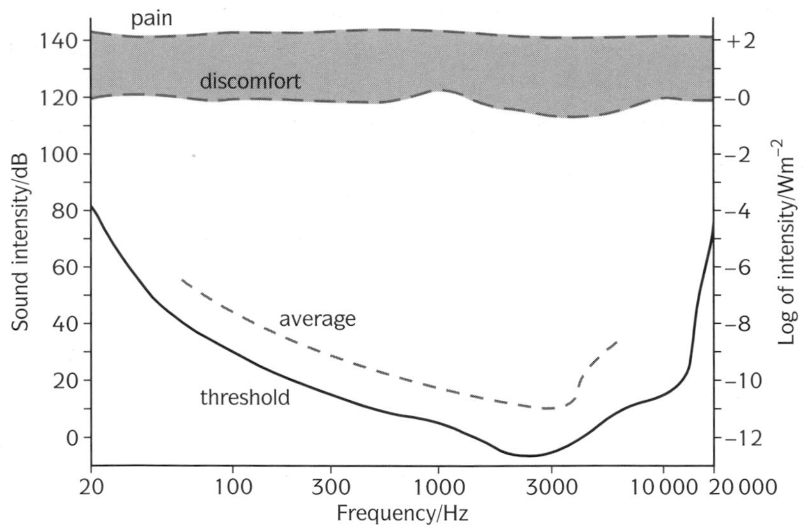

● ***Figure 3.6*** Sensitivity of the human ear. The 'threshold' curve shows the threshold of hearing for a young person with good hearing. The 'average' curve is the average threshold for all people.

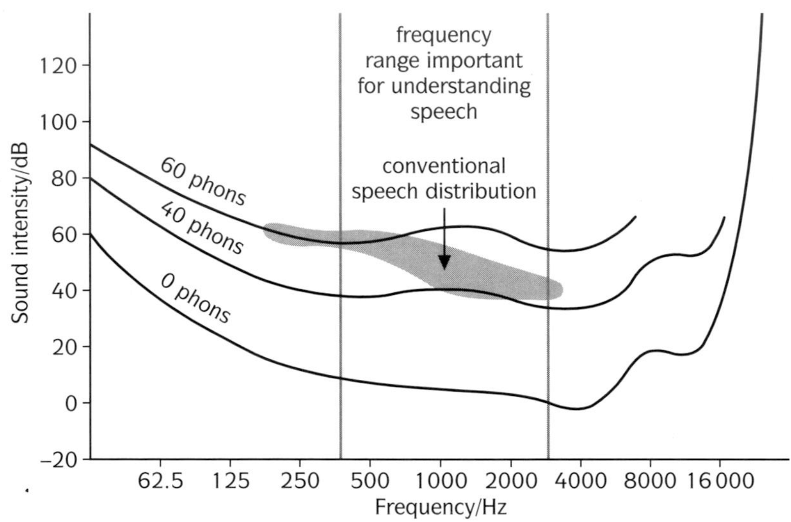

● ***Figure 3.7*** Curves of equal loudness at different sound intensity levels.

Hearing defects

The mechanism of hearing can be thought of as a two-step process. The first step is conduction of sound vibrations through the air or through the bone of the skull. These sound vibrations are transmitted to the oval window of the inner ear and into the perilymph and endolymph. The second step in hearing is the sensing of vibrations in the endolymph by the hair cells and the production of nerve impulses which travel to the brain.

A hearing defect can occur in either step of the process. If it is due to the mechanisms which conduct the vibrations to the inner ear, then it is called **conductive deafness.** If it is due to the sensory mechanisms in the inner ear then it is called **sensorineural deafness.** It is possible for there to be faults of both kinds in the same person.

Conductive deafness may be due to a blockage of the external canal by wax, or the tympanic membrane may be punctured or damaged. In the middle ear, the ossicles may be damaged or stiff and it is possible to replace them with artificial bones. Temporary conductive deafness can be caused by infection in the middle ear, particularly in children.

The most common cause for sensorineural deafness is exposure to excessive noise. There are regulations to protect people who work in noisy environments. Where noise levels are above 80 dB employers must provide noise protection equipment. If the level is above 90 dB then employees must wear ear protection.

Other causes of sensorineural deafness include tumours in the brain, viral infections which damage the auditory nerve and congenital defects. An example of the latter is congenital cochlear deafness which can be caused in a fetus if the mother has rubella (German measles) during pregnancy.

Treatment for sensorineural deafness has been impossible until recently. Cochlear implants can be used to stimulate the auditory nerves with electrical stimuli.

SAQ 3.3

Sounds can be detected by the inner ear when they are transmitted through the bone. The outer and middle ear play no part in this hearing mechanism. A person suffers from hearing loss and it is unclear whether the loss is due to a defect in the inner ear or the middle ear. Suggest how you would be able to test where the hearing damage had occurred.

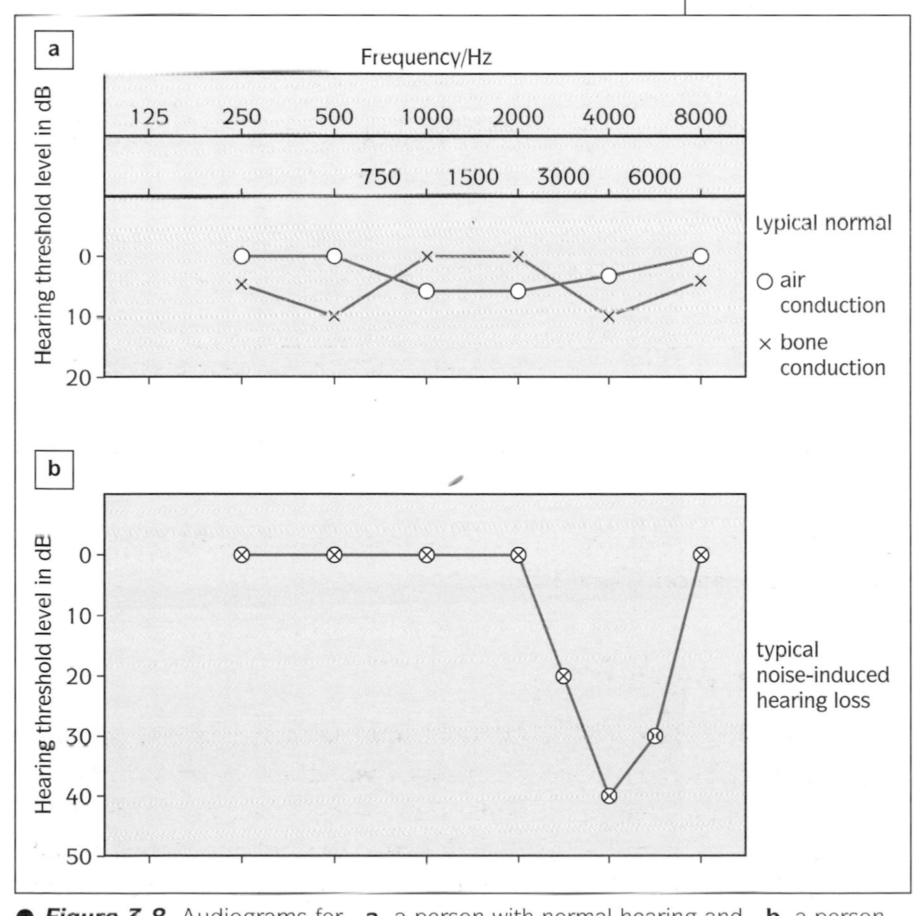

● ***Figure 3.8*** Audiograms for **a** a person with normal hearing and **b** a person with noise-induced hearing loss.

Hearing loss is quite common. About 20% of the adult population have hearing which is substantially impaired, which means that there is a hearing loss of 25 dB over the speech range of 500–2000 Hz.

The measurement of hearing is called **audiometry.** For an adult audiometry test, sounds of six different frequencies are used: 250, 500, 1k, 2k, 4k and 8k Hz. Air conduction is tested by applying the sound through earphones, while bone conduction is tested by a vibrator in contact with the skull near to the ear. The audiometer is calibrated so that the mean intensity level which can just be heard by a group of young adults with no defect is used as the zero level. The sound is increased in intensity until the person who is being tested indicates that they can hear the sound. An audiogram is plotted *(figure 3.8)* which shows hearing loss in decibels against frequency. The graph for a person who has normal hearing would have a straight horizontal line along the zero at the top of the audiogram. Most patients will have hearing below this and the graph showing their response will fall below the zero line. In conductive deafness, air conduction is abnormal and bone conduction normal (because the inner ear still works); in sensorineural deafness, both are abnormal.

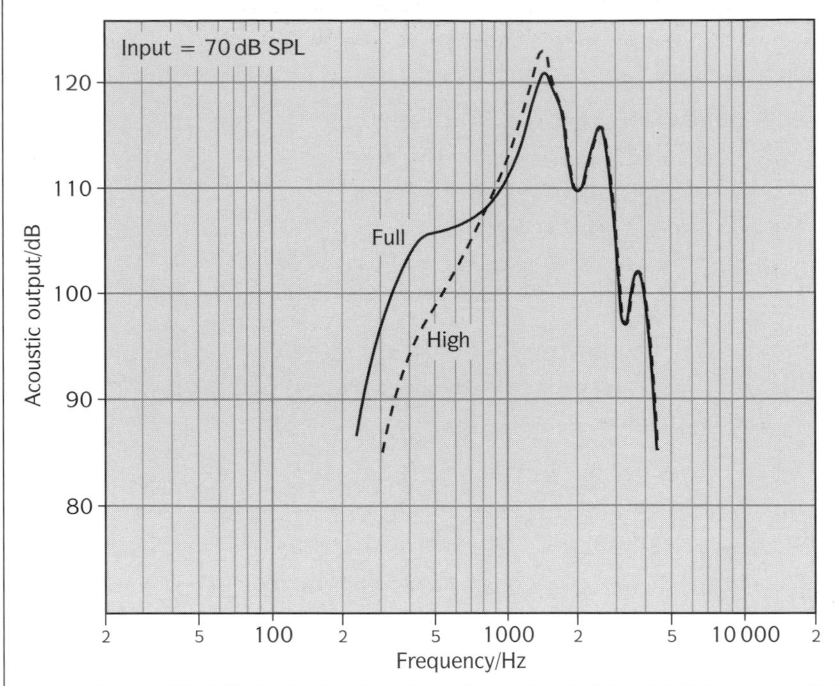

● ***Figure 3.9*** Frequency response of a hearing aid.

Hearing aids

One in four people over 65 will experience some form of hearing loss. This can be remedied, to some extent, by the use of a hearing aid. The normal hearing aid has a microphone which is connected to an amplifier and then to a loudspeaker. An amplification of 90 dB can be obtained. Even though a deaf person may have a hearing threshold of 70–80 dB, their discomfort threshold is the same as that of a person with normal hearing, that is about 100–120 dB. This sets a practical upper limit on the output of the hearing aid. The problem with this simple amplifying system is that it increases all the frequencies that it receives. Normal speech has a range from 400 to 4000 Hz, but hearing loss normally affects the higher frequencies to a greater extent. If all frequencies are amplified equally, when the higher frequencies are boosted to a level where they can be heard, the amplified lower frequencies are also boosted which causes these sounds to distort and cover the high frequencies *(figure 3.9)*.

More recent hearing aids attempt to overcome this problem. They have the ability to process each frequency differently. Some frequencies can be amplified while others are decreased in intensity. This means that speech frequencies can be amplified while traffic sounds can be filtered out. They have the additional advantage that they are very small and can fit into the ear canal. The volume control and switch for the microphone are located on a remote control panel which is the size of a credit card. Each hearing aid is designed to suit the patient receiving it and the entire package can be contained in one piece of plastic moulded to fit that person's ear *(figure 3.10)*.

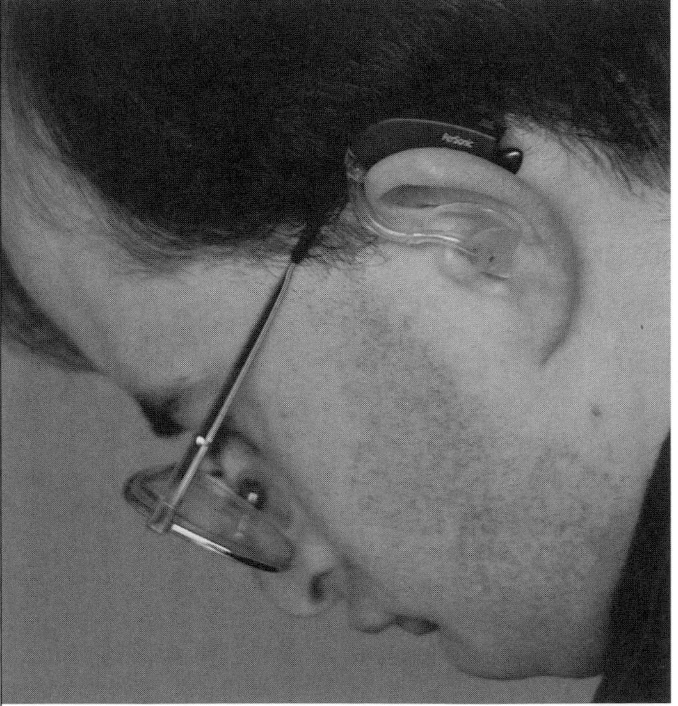

● ***Figure 3.10*** A modern hearing aid.

SUMMARY

- The ear responds to an incoming sound wave by transmitting the vibrations from the outer ear via the pinna to the tympanic membrane and then via the ossicles to the cochlea. Each of these parts transmits the vibrations and increases their power.
- Sensitivity is the response of the ear to changes in intensity, but frequency response is the smallest change in frequency that the ear can detect.
- The threshold of hearing is the minimum intensity that is just audible at a given frequency. Discomfort can occur at 120 dB.
- The ear has a logarithmic response to intensity. This means that small changes of intensity are more easily detected at low intensities.
- Intensity level is measured in bels and is calculated as

$$\text{intensity level} = \log \frac{I}{I_0}$$

The intensity level in decibels is multiplied by 10.

- Loudness is a subjective response to an intensity level.

Questions

1. Describe the three main parts of the ear and explain their contributions to the process of hearing.
2. There are two common causes of hearing loss in adults. Explain what these two types are, how they can be distinguished, their causes and if a hearing aid can help these problems.

The production and detection of ionising radiation

By the end of this chapter you should be able to:

1. recall the mechanisms by which X-rays are absorbed in matter, namely Compton scattering, photoelectric effect and pair production;
2. understand the relative importance of these mechanisms in terms of photon energy and mass number of the target material;
3. describe how a computed tomography (CT) scanner operates;
4. describe how the radioactive isotope technetium-99m is used for diagnostic purposes;
5. describe how technetium-99m is produced;
6. describe how a scintillation counter operates;
7. describe the operation of a rectilinear scanner;
8. describe the structure and typical uses of a gamma camera.

The production of X-rays

X-rays were discovered by Wilhelm Röntgen in 1895. In a modern X-ray tube a high voltage (of about 100 kV) is placed across electrodes in an evacuated tube *(figure 4.1)*. When the negative electrode (cathode) is heated, by an electric current passing through it, electrons are emitted. These electrons are accelerated by the high voltage to hit the positive electrode (anode). When these electrons strike the anode most of their energy is transferred into thermal energy. However, some of the energy causes the emission of X-rays. The greater the voltage across the electrodes, the greater the energy of the X-rays. The energy of a ray or wave is related to the frequency as follows:

$$E = hf,$$

where h (Planck's constant) = 6.63×10^{-34} J s. Hence, as the energy increases the frequency of the X-rays increases, and the wavelength decreases.

To produce X-rays for use in diagnosis, the voltage across the electrodes is held between 80 and 120 kV. For treatment of cancers, the voltage used is greater than 200 kV, to produce X-rays of greater energy.

X-ray photons are produced when a fast-moving stream of electrons is rapidly decelerated in a material of high atomic number. This can be produced in an X-ray tube as shown in *figure 4.2*.

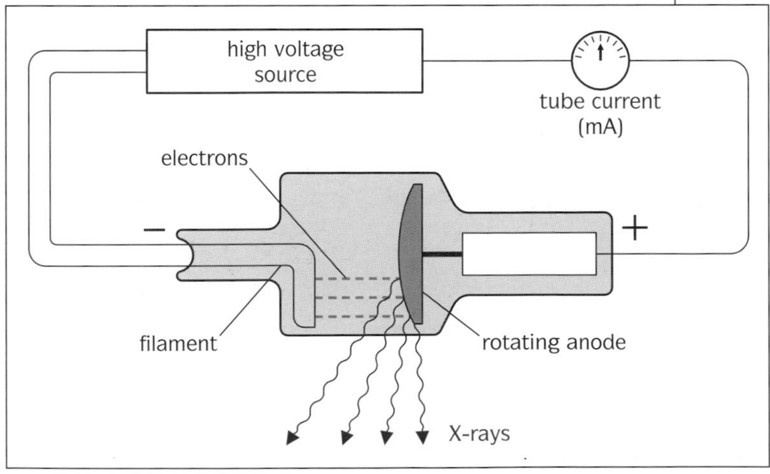

● ***Figure 4.1*** The basic components of an X-ray unit.

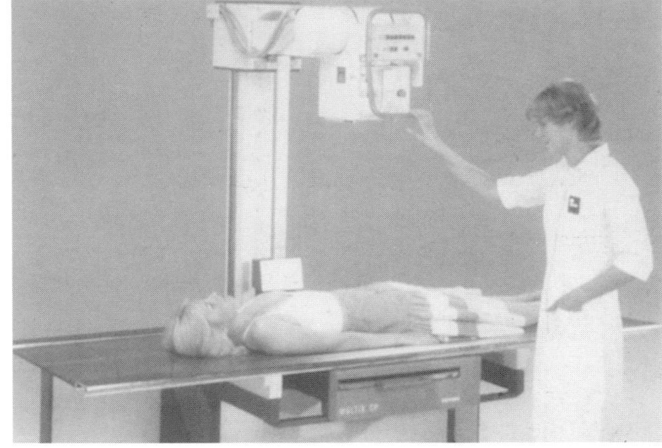

● ***Figure 4.2*** A basic X-ray set.

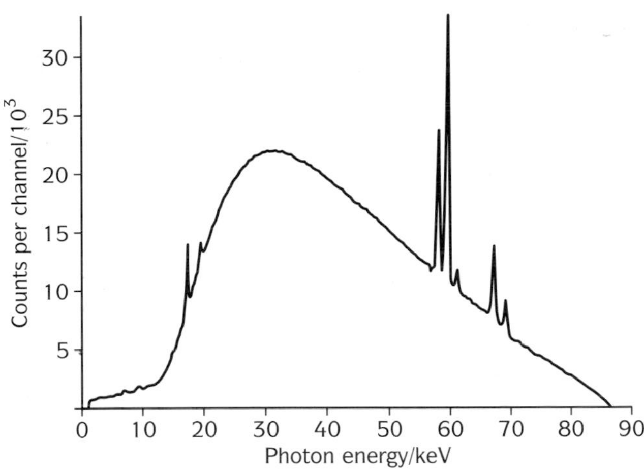

● ***Figure 4.3*** The output spectrum of a typical X-ray tube. The peaks of energy are produced when electrons fall from one orbit to another.

- **Characteristic X-rays,** which have definite energies, are produced when there is a rearrangement of the electrons within the target atoms. These are relatively unimportant in medical applications.
- **Bremsstrahlung** (or braking) **radiation,** is associated with the deflection of the bombarding electrons in the electrostatic field of the target nuclei. Since it is likely that only a fraction of the electrons' energy will be transferred, bremsstrahlung X-rays have a range of energies, the maximum being the energy of the bombarding electrons (that is when all the energy is transferred). The composite output spectrum from a typical X-ray tube is shown in *figure 4.3*.

Absorption of X-rays by matter

Unlike charged particles, X-ray photons do not directly cause ionisation of the matter or tissue through which they pass. The energy of the photons is transferred to kinetic energy in the electrons of the absorbing material and this energy is dissipated in ionisation and excitation.

The absorption of photons is related exponentially to the intensity of the radiation (I) which decreases both with thickness of the absorbing material (x) and with a constant (μ) which is characteristic of the material and of the energy of the photons. The mathematical expression is:

$$I = I_0 \, e^{-\mu x}$$

where I_0 is the intensity of the incident ray. There are three main processes involved in the absorption of X-rays: the photoelectric effect, Compton scattering and pair production.

Photoelectric effect

In the photoelectric effect the incident X-ray photon ejects one of the orbital electrons from an atom of the absorbing material, giving almost all its energy to the electron. This electron then travels through the absorber ionising and exciting other atoms in the material *(figure 4.4)*. The incident photon disappears and an electron from a higher shell may drop down to fill the 'hole' left by the ejected electron with the subsequent emission of a characteristic photon.

In this case the attenuation coefficient, μ, increases in proportion to the cube of the atomic number, Z^3, and reduces in proportion to the cube of the incident photon energy, E^3:

$$\mu \propto Z^3, \ \mu \propto 1/E^3.$$

Compton scattering

In Compton scattering, the incident X-ray photon is scattered by an orbital electron of an atom in the absorbing material *(figure 4.5)*. Some of the energy

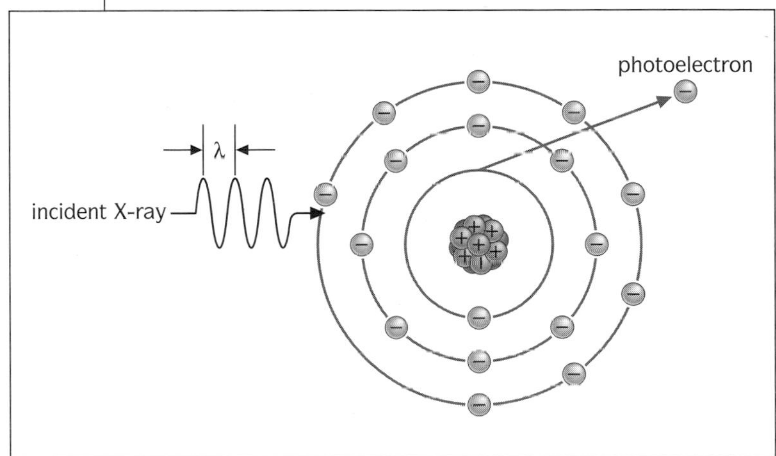

● ***Figure 4.4*** Photoelectric effect.

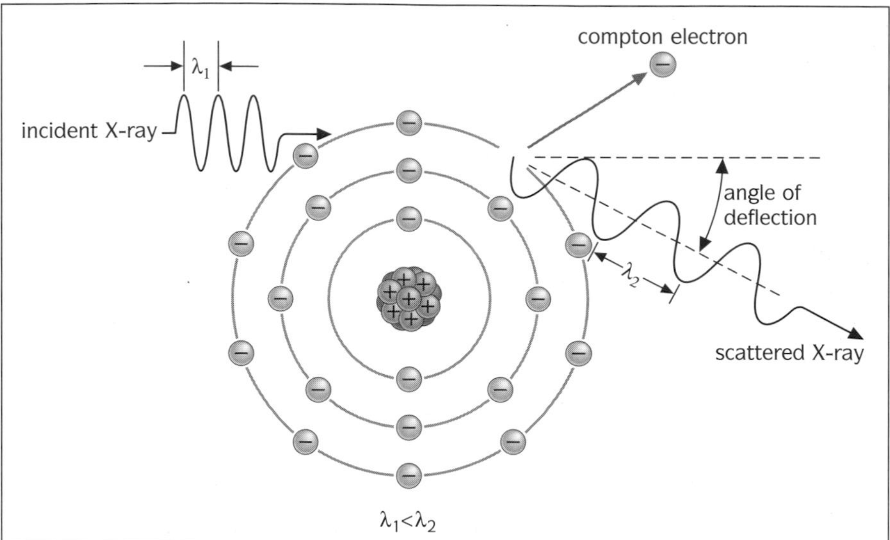

● ***Figure 4.5*** Compton scattering.

is given to the electron that was struck and it goes off in a different direction to the photon. The electron is called a Compton electron and may have any energy from zero up to a maximum of about two-thirds of the incident photon energy. The scattered photon can undergo further scattering processes until it is finally completely absorbed in a photoelectric interaction.

In this case the attenuation coefficient, μ, decreases very gradually with increasing energy, E, and is independent of the atomic number Z:

$$\mu \propto 1/E.$$

Pair production

Pair production occurs at very high photon energies (>1.02 MeV). The incident X-ray photon interacts with the nucleus of an atom. The photon disappears and an electron and positron pair are created *(figure 4.6)*. The energy of these particles is then transferred by ionisation. As it comes to rest, the positron is annihilated by a neighbouring electron to produce two identical photons.

In this case, the attenuation coefficient, μ, increases slowly with E and increases more rapidly in proportion to Z^2:

$$\mu \propto E,\ \mu \propto Z^2.$$

SAQ 4.1

The attenuation coefficients for X-rays in fat, muscle and tumours are similar in value. Why is this a disadvantage in imaging?

At lower incident X-ray photon energies, the photoelectric effect is the most likely of the three processes to happen. As photon energy increases, the Compton scattering effect becomes more common until, at high energies, pair production becomes the most important of the three processes. However, the dependence of attenuation on atomic number has significance when X-ray photons strike tissue. Soft tissue has an average atomic number of 7 due to elements of carbon, hydrogen and oxygen. Bone has an effective atomic number of 14 due to the high proportions of calcium and phosphorus it contains. Since photoelectric absorption increases in proportion to Z^3, this effect is more likely to occur in bone than in soft tissue. In addition, the density of bone is much greater than that of soft tissue which causes greater attenuation of the beam for the same thickness. So bone appears more opaque than soft tissue in X-ray images.

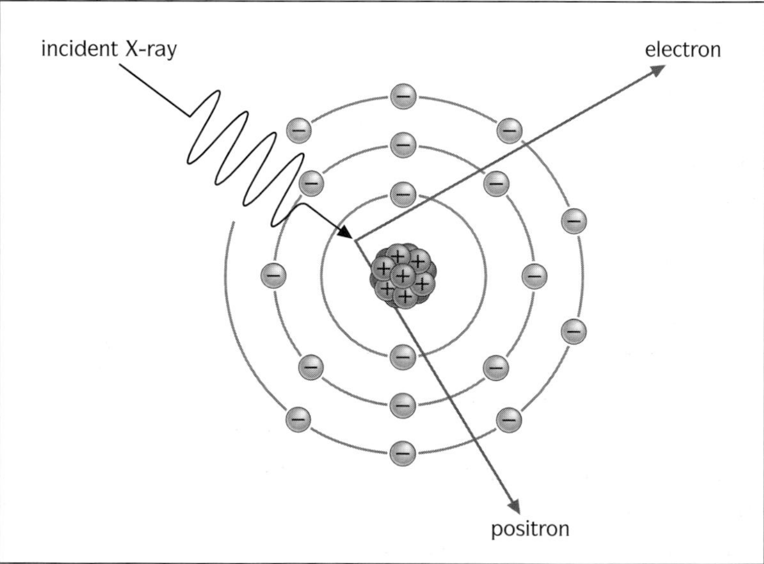

● ***Figure 4.6*** Pair production.

At the lower energies used for imaging for diagnosis, pair production does not occur. The photoelectric effect is more useful than the Compton scattering effect since it allows us to see bones and other heavy materials in the body. At 30 keV bone absorbs X-rays eight times better than tissue. Since the average atomic numbers of different types of soft tissue varies little, there is almost no difference between them in the absorption of X-rays. To make use of the photoelectric effect, contrast media which have high atomic numbers, such as barium and iodine, are used. For example, barium is swallowed and used to outline parts of the gut such as the stomach and intestines; iodine is injected into specific blood vessels to measure blood flow rate through parts of the body.

If the Compton effect was the only process that could be used, then X-rays would have limited usefulness since this effect depends only on the density of materials. Bone has about twice the density of tissue and will be seen on an X-ray image but with low contrast. The Compton effect can also reduce the information on an X-ray image because it reduces contrast and therefore the detail on the image.

SAQ 4.2

In medical diagnosis, in which kinds of cases would X-rays produce the best images?

X-ray detection

Like photographic film, an X-ray film consists of an inert plastic sheet coated with silver halide crystals. Following absorption of radiation, the silver halide molecules are ionised; processing (developing and fixing) turns the silver ions into black silver particles to produce an image. The relationship between the degree of blackening (optical density) and exposure to X-rays is shown in *figure 4.7*. This is known as the **characteristic curve** of the film.

The film is relatively insensitive since most X-rays will pass through the film without interaction. It can be made to record more of the X-rays if it is sandwiched between two sheets containing a phosphor which converts X-rays to visible light, to which the film is more sensitive. Each X-ray photon produces several thousand light photons, though only 10–20% of these are detected. Such intensifier screens permit an image to be obtained with 100–500 times less exposure to radiation.

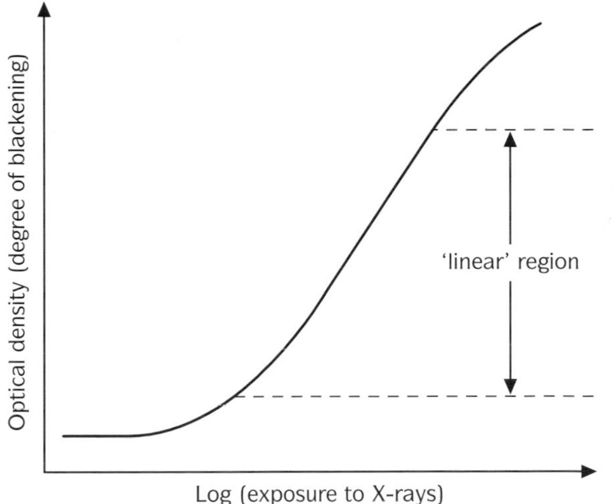

● ***Figure 4.7*** Characteristic curve for X-ray film.

In digital X-ray systems, the most common arrangement is for the X-ray beam to be directed onto an **image intensifier**. This comprises a screen covered by a fluorescent material which is backed by a photocathode. When the X-ray photons hit the screens they are converted first into light photons and then electrons. These electrons are accelerated by an electric field onto a smaller fluorescent screen which is viewed by a television camera. This information is fed into a computer (*figure 4.8*).

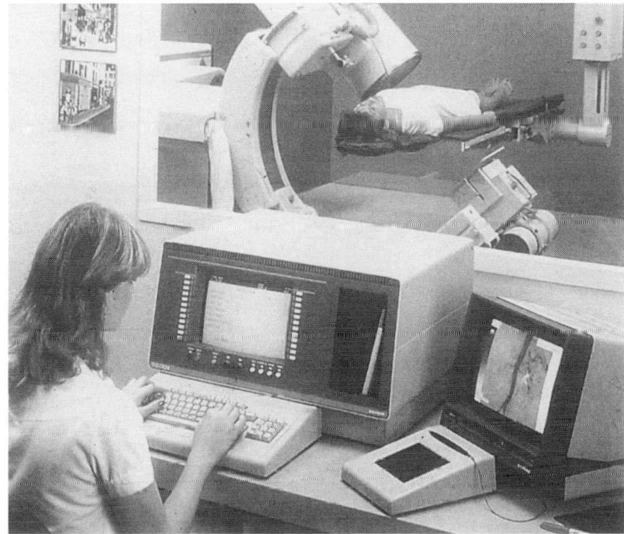

● ***Figure 4.8*** Digital X-ray system.

Computed tomography

Conventional X-ray photographs, or radiographs, are the most common images used in hospitals. However, they have an important limitation because they contain information from all depths in the body superimposed on top of each other. One possible solution is to take a number of X-rays from different angles from which the radiologist can work out which parts of the image correspond to which part of each organ. This is a rather difficult and time-consuming process.

In 1971 Geoffrey Hounsfield and his colleagues at EMI in the UK developed a machine to overcome these problems, the computerised axial tomographic scanner or CAT (or CT) scanner. The first scanner's operation is shown in *figure 4.9*. An X-ray tube and detector were mounted on a gantry which was free to scan across and around the patient. A narrow pencil-thin X-ray beam was used to obtain the finest detail. At each position, a measurement of the amount of radiation transmitted through the patient was made. Each scan was made by moving the tube and detector across the patient and then rotating the gantry by a few degrees. The process was repeated until the machine had made one complete revolution of the patient.

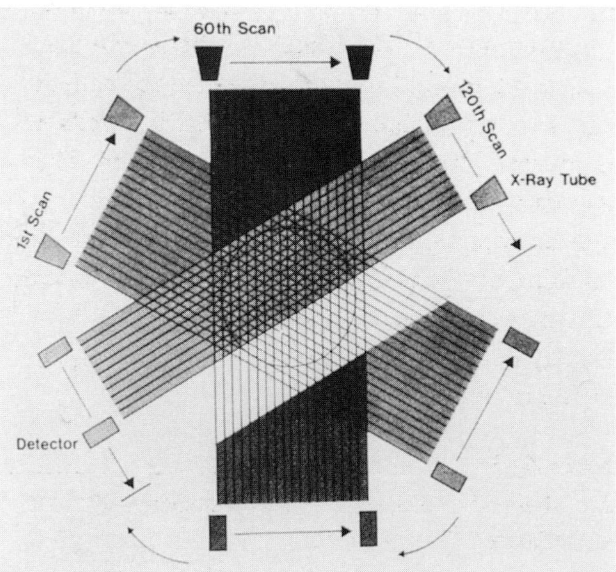

● ***Figure 4.9*** Operation of the first computerised axial tomographic (CT) scanner.

These early scanners showed that the technique could work but the scans took 10 to 15 minutes to complete. In the very first scans the patient had to be surrounded by water-filled bags to make the length of material that the X-ray beam passed through equal in all directions. This can now be corrected for by the computer program.

Modern scanners can collect the data in a few seconds. They use a fan-shaped X-ray beam and a complete ring of 720 detectors. In these scanners only the X-ray tube rotates *(figure 4.10)*. The total number of readings of intensity will vary from 200 000 to 500 000. If the patient moves while the tube rotates, the image will be fuzzy, so the patient is advised to hold their breath. In the latest scanners, the tube makes several rotations while the patient bed moves through the gantry. This means that the X-ray beam effectively moves in a spiral pattern along the patient's body and information about a whole volume is obtained.

The information from these scans, as intensity measurements, is then processed by the computer to obtain the final image. The process usually used is called back projection and involves many million arithmetical computations.

SAQ 4.3

What are the main advantages of CT compared to conventional X-rays?

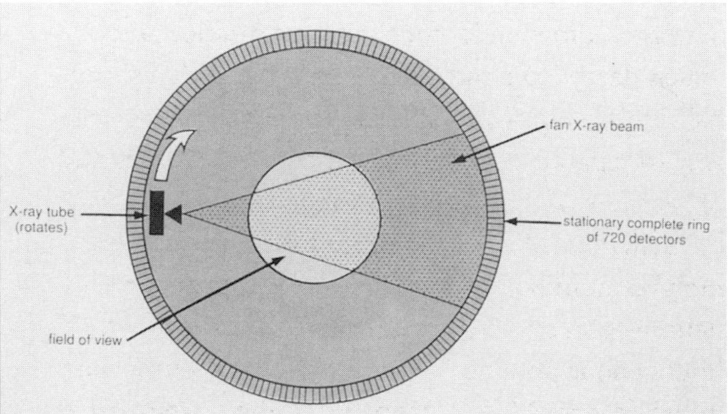

● ***Figure 4.10*** How a modern CT scanner works.

Gamma radiation in nuclear medicine

Nuclear medicine is the use of radioactive materials in medicine, both for diagnosis (chapter 5) and therapy (chapter 6). In therapy, the aim is to localise the radioactive material in diseased cells so that they are killed by the radiation. Since the normal cells surrounding the diseased tissue must not be killed, short-range radiations (alpha and beta) are used.

In diagnosis, radioactive materials are used to study the function of organs. The materials used are **radiopharmaceuticals** which comprise pharmaceuticals (chemicals used in medicine) and a radionuclide. The pharmaceutical used will depend on the organ which is to be studied, while the radionuclide makes it possible to monitor the passage of the radiopharmaceutical through parts of the body. The radionuclide needs to be a gamma emitter so that it can be monitored from outside the patient (see chapter 6) and should have a reasonably short half-life to limit the radiation dose to the patient. The radionuclide most commonly used is technetium-99m (m means meta-stable).

Technetium-99m

If the radionuclide had a long half-life, the patient would be subjected to a high radiation dose. A short half-life, such as the 6 h half-life of technetium-99m, limits the radiation dose but has problems because of the time required to transport the radionuclide from the production site to the hospital. One solution to this problem is to use a long-lived 'parent' radionuclide, for the transportation stage, which decays to a radioactive material with a short half-life for use with patients. There must be an easy way to separate the two so that the patient does not receive any of the parent radionuclide.

Technetium-99m is produced from molybdenum-99. Molybdenum-99 decays to technetium-99m by beta emission with a half-life of 67 hours and is obtained from a nuclear reactor. The molybdenum-99 is transported to the hospital in a generator *(figure 4.11)* which comprises a saline reservoir, an alumina column onto which the molybdenum is adsorbed (as ammonium molybdenate), and a filter which sterilises material passing through it and prevents the passage of any alumina particles out of the generator. The column is shielded with lead (or depleted uranium) to reduce the radiation dose to the user.

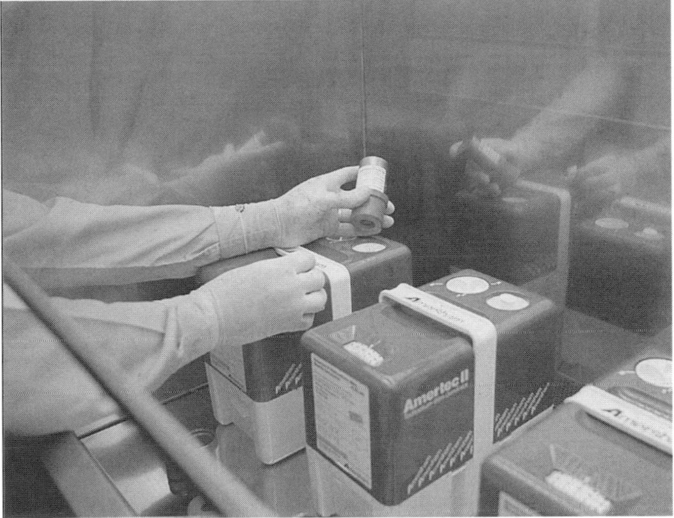

● ***Figure 4.11*** Technetium generator.

Procedure

Saline solution is passed through the column onto which the molybdenum is adsorbed; the technetium is soluble in saline but molybdenum is not. This process is known as **elution** and results in a solution of sodium pertechnetate which is collected in an output vial. The content of the output vial can be diluted and split into a number of patient doses. The total amount of radioactivity available is governed by the half-life of molybdenum. The generator is eluted daily until the radioactive concentration falls to a level which is too low to be useful, which happens after two or three half-lives (that is 2 or 3 × 67 hours). This means that a weekly delivery of a generator to hospital departments is necessary.

SAQ 4.4

a What is the advantage of using technetium-99m as a radioactive isotope in medicine?

b Why is the design of the generator useful in a hospital for a number of patients?

Scintillation detectors

Some materials, when they absorb ionising radiation, produce secondary electrons by the photoelectric, Compton scattering and pair production processes that generate photons of light. These materials are called **scintillators**. The light is emitted in a short pulse or flash and the amplitude of the pulse is directly proportional to the energy absorbed so that scintillators can be used to measure the level of ionising radiation absorbed. If a material of a high atomic number is used, the sensitivity is increased.

Solid scintillators

The most common material used as a scintillator is sodium iodide which is activated by the addition of a small amount of thallium. Sodium iodide produces a very large amount of light compared to other scintillators. It takes about 10 ns for the light to reach its maximum after the ionising radiation is absorbed.

The scintillator is contained in a thin aluminium can, to prevent light entering from outside. The can is sealed to keep moisture out because sodium iodide is hygroscopic, that is it absorbs water from the atmosphere. The inside of the can is coated with powdered titanium dioxide, which acts as a reflector to direct all the light from the scintillator through a quartz or plexiglass window in the rear of the can.

The light output from the window is directed into a **photomultiplier**. This is a sealed evacuated glass tube which contains a series of electrodes. The inner surface of the front of the photomultiplier is coated with a photoemissive material which absorbs the photons and re-emits the energy in the form of electrons, as in the photoelectric effect.

These electrons are then accelerated by a DC voltage to the first electrode. Each incident electron causes the emission of two or three electrons which are accelerated in turn to the next electrode where the process is repeated. The last electrode produces the final output pulse which is by now a cascade of electrons *(figure 4.12)*. A typical photomultiplier has a gain of between 10^4 and 10^6 and the potential difference between successive electrodes is about 100 V.

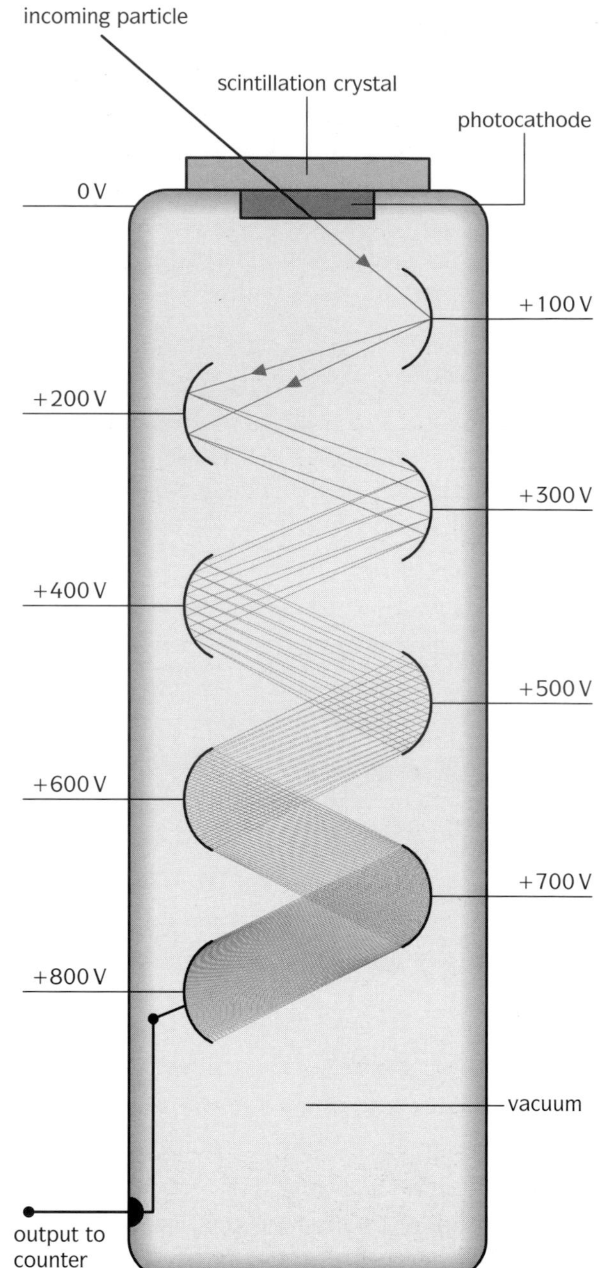

● ***Figure 4.12*** Scintillation counter showing cascade of electrons.

The main use of scintillation detectors is in nuclear medicine, where the gamma radiation comes from a radioactive material inside the body. The gamma rays pass through tissue easily and are detected outside the body by a scintillation detector in a device such as a rectilinear scanner or gamma camera.

Rectilinear scanners

Rectilinear scanners were developed in 1950 and were the first instruments used to image automatically a gamma-emitting radionuclide from within the body. The detector is a sodium iodide crystal fitted with a lead shield and collimator to detect gamma rays up to 500 keV. The collimator is a block of lead pierced by an array of tapered holes, focused on a point several centimetres in front of the collimator face. This allows the detection of a large proportion of those gamma rays that are emitted from the point of the body at the focus.

At each point of the body, the intensity recorded is proportional to the radiation count rate detected. The position on the display corresponds to the position of the detector in space. The image is built up by passing the detector over the body in a series of lines, similar to the image that is built up on a television screen *(figure 4.13)*.

Rectilinear scanners have important limitations:

- most scanners can only scan in horizontal planes;
- it takes a long time to build up the image which is a particular problem when the distribution of the radioactive material in the body is changing over time.

Very few of these instruments are now in use, since they have been superseded by the gamma camera.

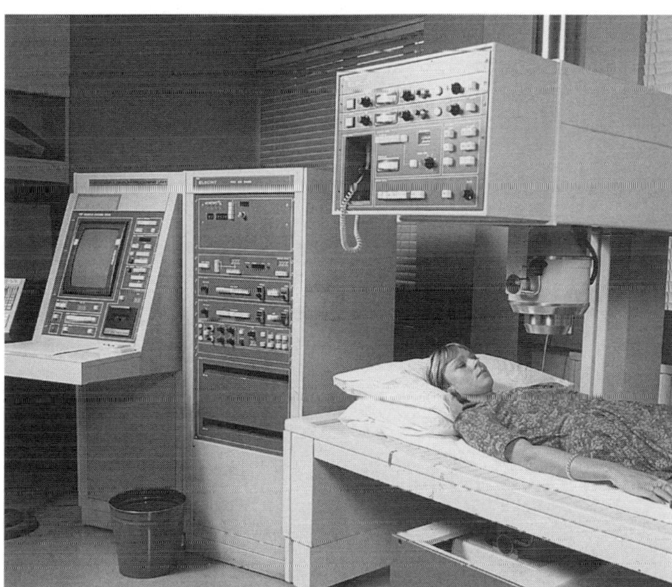

● ***Figure 4.13*** Rectilinear scanner.

The gamma camera

The gamma camera was first developed in 1957 by Hal Anger in the United States. It is the major imaging device in use now in diagnostic nuclear medicine.

The camera uses a single, very large sodium iodide crystal, typically between 400 and 500 mm in diameter and 9–12 mm thick. This crystal is viewed by a large number of photomultipliers arranged in concentric hexagonal rings around a central tube *(figure 4.14)*. The field of view is limited by a collimator which is a block of lead that has up to 35 000 holes. The usual parallel-hole collimator only allows photons which travel perpendicular to the crystal to pass through.

A gamma photon reaching the crystal may interact to give a light flash which will be detected by the photomultipliers. The intensity of light reaching a given photomultiplier will be inversely related to the square of its distance from the point of interaction. By processing the differing amplitudes of signals from all the photomultipliers, it is possible to work out where in the crystal the light pulse originated. By adding all the photomultiplier outputs, a signal is obtained which depends on the energy of the gamma photon detected.

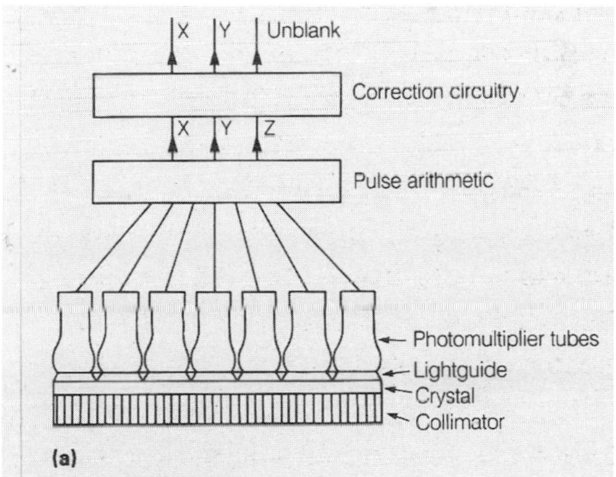

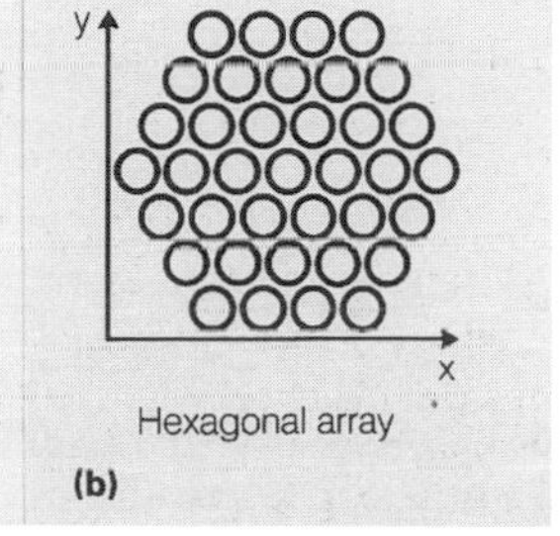

● ***Figure 4.14*** Arrangement of photo multipliers in a gamma camera. (a) Schematic cross section (b) plan view of photomultipliers.

It is usual to analyse this signal to select events which correspond to photoelectric absorption only. Signals corresponding to Compton scattering are rejected because it is not possible to determine whether the scattering occurred in the patient's body or in the detector. If it occurred in the patient's body, the event would be placed in an incorrect location.

For signals corresponding to photoelectric absorption, the positional co-ordinates of the event are used to generate a dot on an oscilloscope. The image of the distribution of the radioactive material in the body is obtained by making a time exposure photograph of the oscilloscope. This usually contains between 2×10^5 and 5×10^5 dots.

Different collimators can be used with different numbers and sizes of holes *(figure 4.15)*. A smaller number of larger holes will increase the sensitivity of the detector but will reduce the definition or ability to see detail. The thickness of the lead block can also affect the sensitivity.

The energies of the gamma rays will also affect the final image. If the energy is too high, the gamma rays will pass through the crystal and will not be absorbed by it. At low energies, the rays will be scattered within the patient and the final image will be poor. In addition, the patient will absorb an increased dose of radiation.

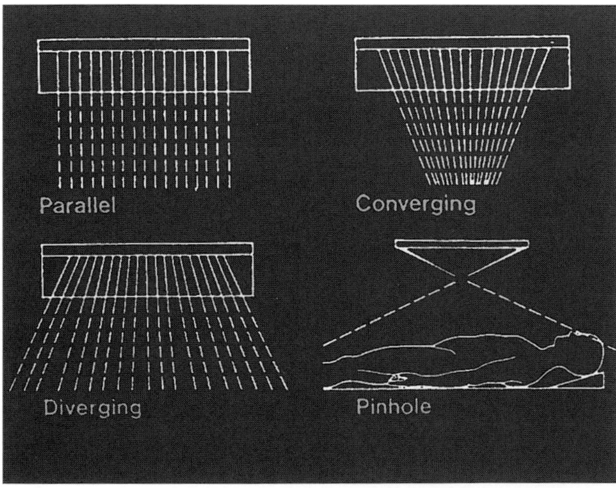

● ***Figure 4.15*** Different collimator types.

An alternative means of storing the data is to send the information about the x and y co-ordinates of each event directly to a computer, to generate a digital image which can then be processed.

Cross-sectional images of the distribution of the radioactive material in the body can be obtained by rotating the gamma camera around the patient to give planar images from a number of angles (usually 64 or 128). These images are then used as the input to a computer which combines the images to produce a three-dimensional image. This information can also be displayed as 'slices' through the body. This technique is known as single photon emission computed tomography (SPECT).

SAQ 4.5

The above devices are classes of scintillation devices.

a What is meant by a scintillation device?

b Explain what effect the number of holes in a collimator can have on the final image.

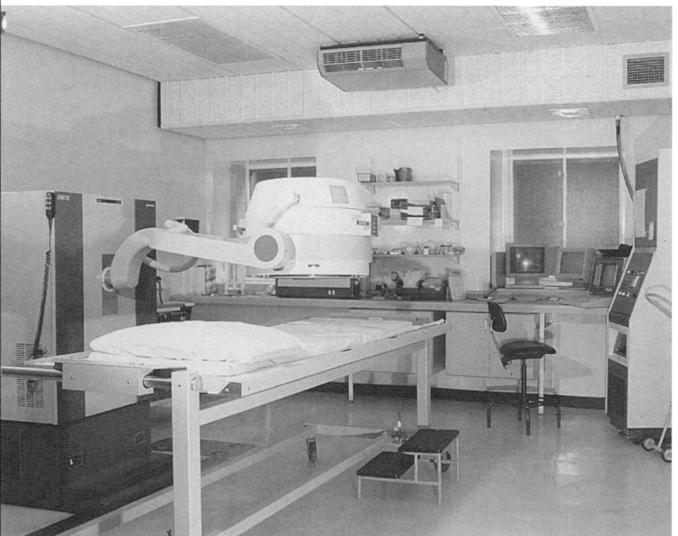

● ***Figure 4.16*** Gamma camera.

SUMMARY

- There are three main methods by which X-rays are attenuated in matter: the photoelectric effect, Compton scattering and pair production.

  Each method will vary in attenuation according to the atomic number of atoms in the absorbing material and with the energy of the incident photon.
- X-rays can be detected using photographic film. Intensifier screens permit an image to be obtained with 100–500 times less exposure to radiation. Digital X-ray systems display the image on a fluorescent screen.
- CT scanners operate by using an X-ray tube and detectors which can rotate around the patient. The use of a computer to process the information results in a three-dimensional image.
- Nuclear medicine is the use of radioactive materials in medicine. The most commonly used radionuclide is technetium-99m, which is a gamma emitter with a half-life of 6 hours. It is produced by decay from molybdenum-99.
- Scintillation detectors operate by using the ionising radiation detected by crystals to produce pulses of light. This light energy is then detected by a photomultiplier which can change the light into an electrical signal and amplify it.
- Rectilinear scanners were the first instruments used to image automatically a gamma-emitting radionuclide from within the body. They can only scan in horizontal planes and it takes a long time to build up an image. They are now mostly replaced with gamma cameras.
- Gamma cameras detect the gamma radiation emitted from a radioactive chemical inside the body. The technique can be used for static or for dynamic studies.

Questions

1 Describe the three main mechanisms by which X-rays interact with matter.

2 Describe the different methods of X-ray detection used in hospitals and their advantages.

Medical imaging

By the end of this chapter you should be able to:

1 describe why non-invasive techniques of diagnosis are important;

2 explain how ultrasonic waves are produced by piezo-electric transducers;

3 describe how ultrasound can be used to obtain images of structures inside the body;

4 describe the use of nuclear medicine in diagnosis;

5 describe how magnetic resonance techniques can be used to image the body;

6 describe and explain the uses of lasers in diagnosis.

In hospitals, a large amount of time and money is spent on producing medical images of various types. A typical hospital will generate over half a million images a year. Worldwide, the number of images produced in medicine comes second only to that produced by satellites. The most common image is still the standard radiograph, but other techniques such as X-ray computed tomography (CT) (page 38), nuclear medicine, ultrasound, nuclear magnetic resonance imaging (MRI), thermography and fibre optic probes are also used. Some of these techniques are described in this chapter.

The majority of these techniques are described as **non-invasive** since they do not require surgery on the patient to produce the image. This means that there is a much lower risk to the patient involved in the examination. Some techniques make use of radiation, either transmitted through the patient from an external source (X-rays, ultrasound) or emitted from within the patient, naturally (thermography) or from an internal source (nuclear medicine). Some techniques will involve 'perturbing' the system, for example where a contrast agent is injected to make the structures in the image clearer or where the patient takes exercise, as in studies of the heart and circulatory system.

Radiography

Conventional radiography is based upon the differential attenuation of X-rays by the different tissues of the body as the radiation beam passes through them. The differing amounts of radiation reaching the film or detector are recorded and form an image. As noted in chapter 4, low energy X-rays are used for diagnostic imaging, where the photoelectric effect dominates. Since several types of body tissue have almost the same average atomic number, they produce very little difference in attenuation. So, on the final image, there is little contrast between them to make them visible. In such cases, **contrast agents** are used. These are usually materials of very high atomic number, such as iodine and barium. For example, liquids containing iodine can be injected into selected blood vessels to study blood flow, and barium can be swallowed to outline the stomach and intestines *(figure 5.1)*.

Digital systems are used in radiography primarily in subtraction techniques in which an image of a structure, such as the arrangement of blood vessels in the kidney, is compared with another image of the same structure after it was

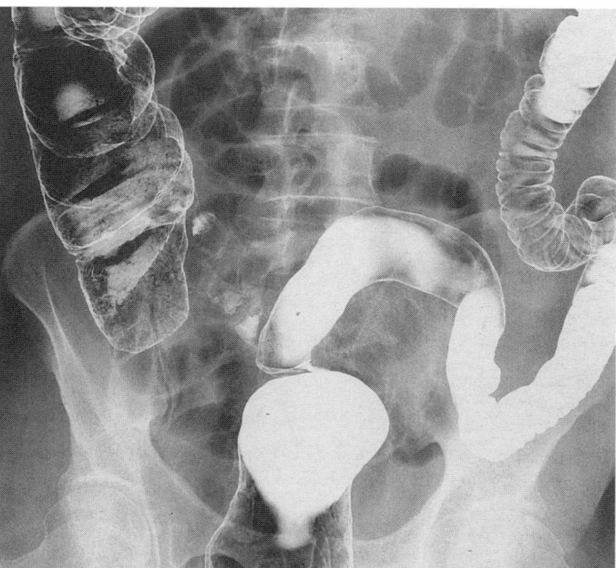

● ***Figure 5.1*** X-ray photograph of gut using barium as contrast material to show detail.

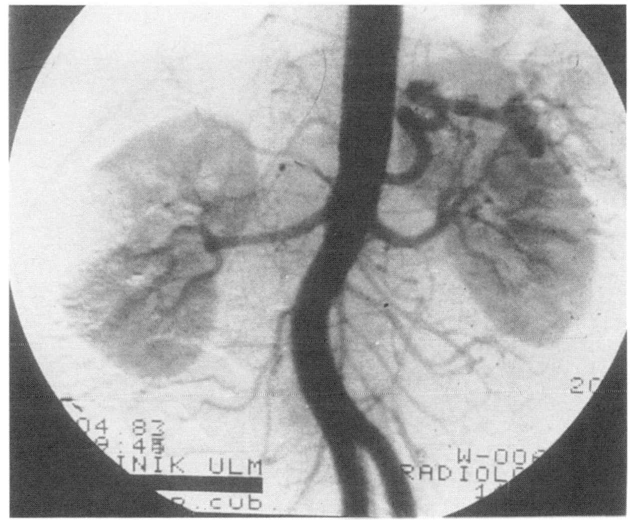

● **Figure 5.2** X-ray photograph of blood vessels in the kidney using the subtraction technique.

injected with a contrast medium. The first image is subtracted from the second to give a resulting image which contains details only of the blood vessels which contained the contrast medium *(figure 5.2)*. This is a very powerful technique and permits the imaging of small structures. Modern computing techniques can even correct for patient motion between the two images.

As described on page 38, CT scanners can produce information that shows quite small differences in tissue density and also the depth of the particular structure *(figure 5.3)*. CT scans can also be produced very quickly. A typical example of their use would be to determine the precise

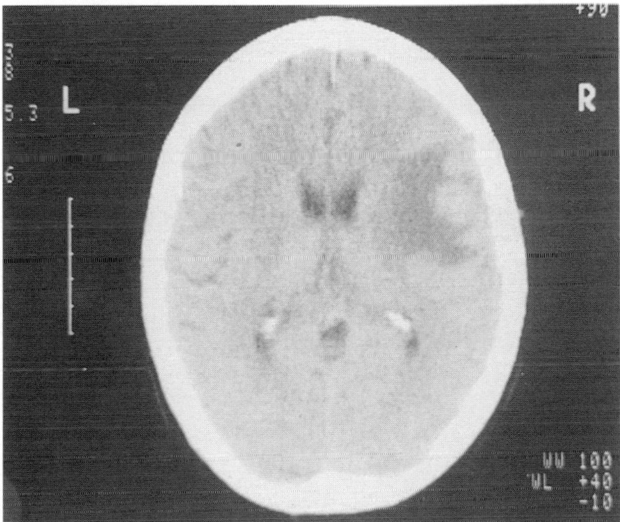

● **Figure 5.3** CT scan of the brain, showing an abnormality on the right side.

location of a head injury following a traffic or a sporting accident. In such cases the exact position of the injury has to be determined quickly. Other possible cases are where the treatment of a brain tumour involves the precise location and size of the tumour. Again a conventional X-ray would not provide this kind of detailed information.

Ultrasound

The normal range of hearing is from 20 to 20 000 Hz and frequencies above this range are called **ultrasound**. Typical frequencies used in medicine are in the megahertz range. The ultrasonic waves are emitted from a transducer which is a device that changes energy from one form to another. This transducer is a crystal which exhibits the **piezoelectric effect**, that is when a potential difference is placed across the crystal it expands along one axis and, when the potential difference is reversed, the crystal contracts. If an alternating potential difference is used, the crystal will oscillate rather like a loudspeaker *(figure 5.4)*. The reverse process is also true: if pressure is applied to the crystal, a small potential difference is formed across the crystal. The transducer thus acts both as

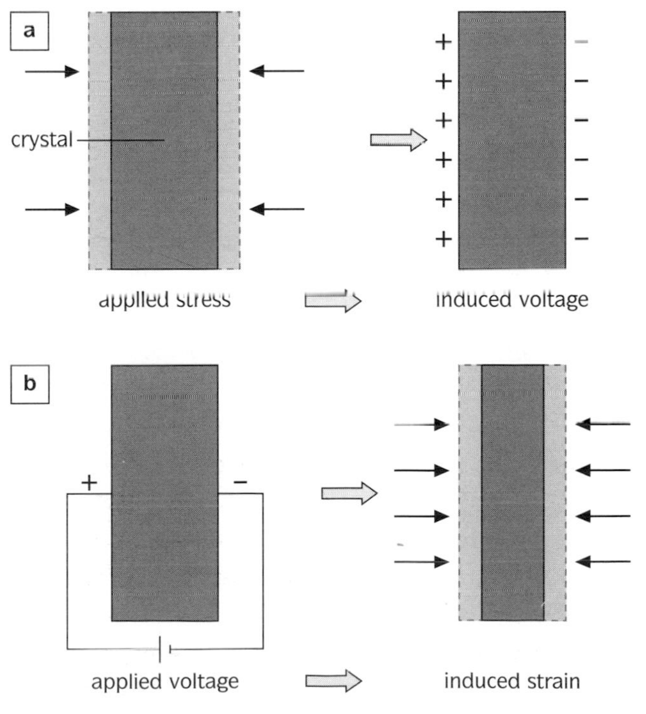

● **Figure 5.4** The piezoelectric effect.

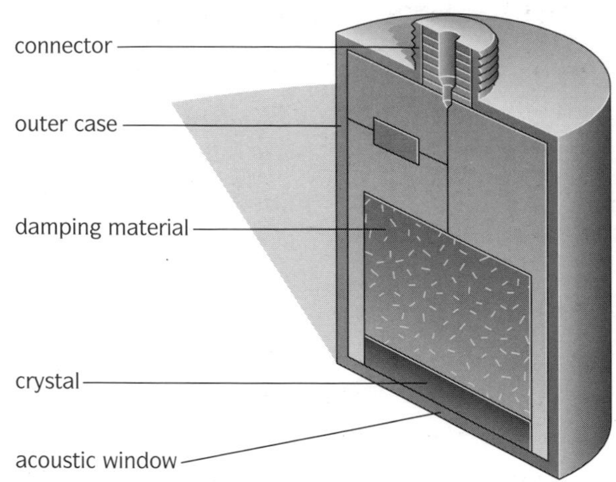

● ***Figure 5.5*** Structure of a transducer.

a transmitter and receiver.

The structure of the transducer has certain key components *(figure 5.5)*. The outer case supports and protects the crystal. The face is a protective acoustic window that is designed to match the electrical characteristics of the crystal and transmit the ultrasound. It is important that the source of the ultrasound is not allowed to reverberate, rather like a bell continuing to ring, and so a damping material (usually epoxy resin) is included. Various materials have been used for the crystal, including quartz and lead zirconate titanate. Modern systems use polyvinylidine difluoride.

The basic ultrasound system works on a pulse echo technique using the equation:

$$s = vt$$

where s is the distance from the transducer to the object and back, v is the speed of sound and t is the time for the sound to travel to the object and return. If the speed of sound in the different substances between the transducer and object is known and the time interval between pulse and reflected signal can be measured, then the distance travelled by the pulse can be calculated.

When a sound wave strikes a boundary between two substances, some of the energy will be reflected and some will be refracted *(figure 5.6)*. The amount of refraction will depend on the **acoustic impedance** of each material, which is given the symbol Z and is defined as:

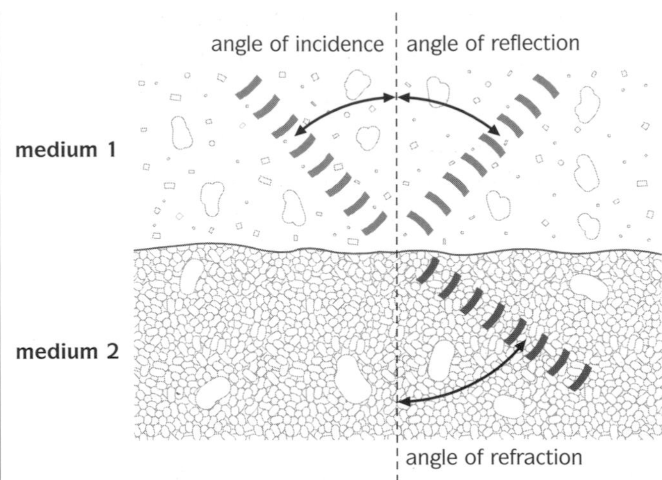

● ***Figure 5.6*** How ultrasound behaves at a boundary between two different tissues. The angle of incidence and the angle of reflection are equal. The angle of refraction depends on the velocity of the ultrasound in each medium.

$$Z = \rho v$$

where ρ is the density of the substance and v is the speed of sound in the substance. The greater the difference in acoustic impedance between the two materials, the greater is the reflected portion of the incident pulse. It can be shown that, for normal incidence (when the ultrasound pulse hits the boundary at right angles), the ratio of the reflected intensity I_r to the initial intensity I_0 is given as

$$\frac{I_r}{I_0} = \frac{[Z_2 - Z_1]^2}{[Z_2 + Z_1]^2}$$

where Z_1 is the acoustic impedance of material 1 and Z_2 is that of material 2.

Material	*Speed of sound* $/\mathrm{m\,s^{-1}}$	*Density* $/\mathrm{kg\,m^{-3}}$	*Acoustic impedance* $/\mathrm{kg\,m^{-2}s^{-1}} \times 10^6$
air	330	1.3	0.0004
bone	2700–4100	$1.3–1.9 \times 10^3$	7.8
muscle	1545–1630	1.0×10^3	1.7
soft tissue	1460–1615	1.0×10^3	1.6
fat	1450	1.0×10^3	1.4
blood	1570	1.0×10^3	1.6

● ***Table 5.1***

Information about different substances and their acoustic impedances are given in *table 5.1*.

Values of the ratios of intensities show that:

air to fat gives a ratio of I_r/I_0 of 0.99,
fat to muscle gives a ratio of 1×10^{-2},
muscle to bone gives a ratio of 0.4.

These figures explain why:

- ultrasound is almost completely reflected at an air–tissue boundary;
- a large amount is reflected at a bone–tissue interface;
- very little ultrasound is reflected at a muscle–tissue boundary.

So, if there is air between the transducer and the skin, very little ultrasound will enter the body. The transducer is therefore 'coupled' to the skin by a gel whose acoustic impedance is similar to that of the skin. Likewise, little can be seen beyond the lungs or any other gas-filled cavities; so the bladder must be full during examination and gas in the intestines avoided by careful positioning of the transducer. Also, nothing can be seen beyond bone, and reflections within bone will create difficulties in interpreting the image. This means that appropriate positioning is required to view the heart (through a gap between the ribs), and detailed examination of the adult brain is not possible.

The **resolution**, that is the detail that can be seen, improves with increasing frequency of the ultrasound, so it might be thought that the clearest pictures would be seen when the highest frequency (and therefore the lowest wavelength) is used. However, the amount of energy that is transferred as heat as the wave passes through tissue increases as frequency increases. To achieve a good image of the organ being investigated, a compromise will be made so that the highest frequency is used that gives the best penetration of the tissues betweeen the transducer and the organ. At the optimum frequency, the beam will reach the organ being investigated in no more than 200 wavelengths.

SAQ 5.1

Calculate the ratio of I_r/I_0 for muscle to soft tissue and explain the significance of the result.

Medical uses of ultrasound

Ultrasound is most commonly used to produce image scans of the body. There are several different types of scan which can be used, depending on the particular organ which is to be studied. These are called the A scan, the B scan and the Doppler scan.

A scan

This is the simplest type of scanner and is still used in some situations. A pulse generator is connected to the ultrasound transducer and the time base of an oscilloscope. The time base is connected to the x plates of the oscilloscope. The output of the receiver in the transducer is amplified and connected to the y plates of the oscilloscope. At the start of each sweep, the pulse generator will send a pulse to the oscilloscope and at the same time trigger the transducer to send an ultrasound pulse into the tissue. When the ultrasound pulse hits a boundary between two different tissue types, some of the signal is reflected back to the receiver where it is amplified and shown as a second pulse on the oscilloscope screen. The distance between the pulses on the x axis will be proportional to the time taken for the pulse to travel to the tissue boundary and back. The amplitude of the received signal will depend on the attenuation of the signals in the materials through which the ultrasound passes and the acoustic impedance of any boundaries it passes through. The attenuation means that the signals received from two interfaces between the same materials at different depths will be different. In imaging, however, the signal from a given interface should be the same irrespective of position. In order to achieve this, signals from deeper in the body are amplified progressively, a process known as **swept gain**. An A scan is a sequence of individual echoes due to reflections along one direction only. This is shown in *figure 5.7*. This type of scan is used to determine the thickness of the eye lens.

B scan

To obtain an image, the B scan uses sensors attached to the probe which can define the

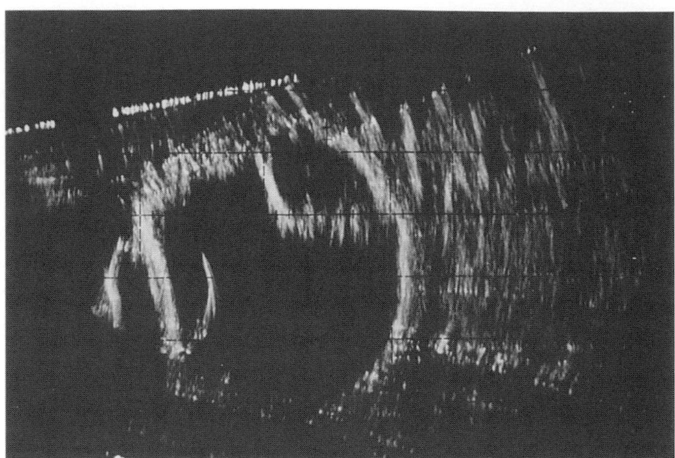

● ***Figure 5.7*** An A scan to determine the thickness of the eye lens.

position and orientation of the organ in a two-dimensional plane. A dot is placed on the screen of a storage oscilloscope representing the calculated position of the reflecting surface. The intensity of the dot is dependent on the amplitude of the echo pulse. The ultrasound beam is 'swept' across the plane and the image built up from the superimposition of a collection of A scans *(figure 5.8)*. Since this takes several seconds, any movements within the organ will degrade the quality of the image. For example it would be difficult to examine pulsating arteries with this method. This can be overcome using 'real time' scanners, which are of two types – phased arrays and sector scanners.

The **phased array scanner** has several small transducers which are triggered individually very close together, with a small phase difference between each. This produces a composite ultrasound scan which does not need the sensors to define the orientation of the beam. The arc covered by the beam from the transducers can be up to 90°.

Sector scanners use one or more transducers which are scanned mechanically across an arc of some 60°. In the single transducer design, the transducer is rocked back and forth which puts a high degree of mechanical strain on the components. More commonly, four transducers are mounted at 90° intervals on a rotating wheel. This is a simpler arrangement mechanically, but requires careful matching of the transducers to obtain the same performance from each.

Phased array and sector scanners are both small hand-held probes and scan fast enough for the images to be viewed as a 'film' on a television screen. The greatest use of these types of scan is during pregnancy to check on the progress of the fetus *(figure 5.9)*. Measurements of the size of the fetus can be made and problems diagnosed at an early stage.

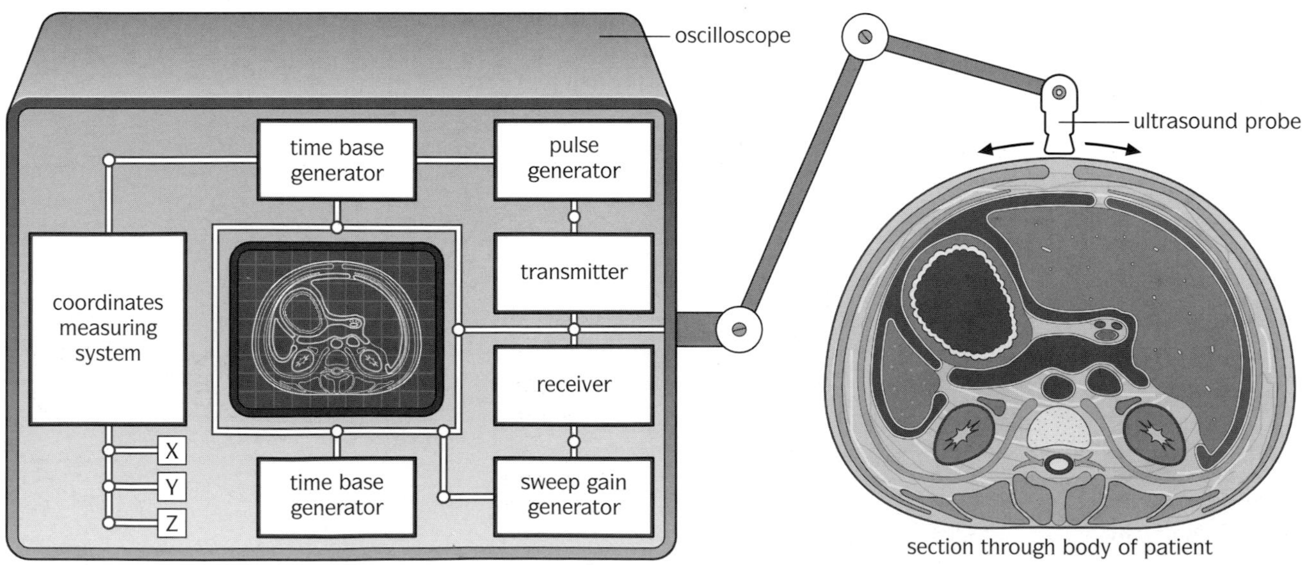

● ***Figure 5.8*** Obtaining a B scan of a section through the body of a patient.

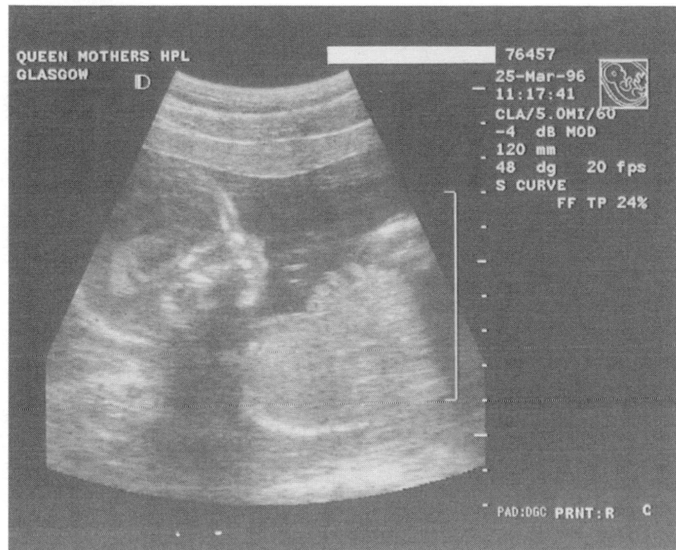

● ***Figure 5.9*** Ultrasound scan of fetus.

SAQ 5.2

Why is an ultrasound B scan used to examine the fetus rather than X-rays?

Doppler ultrasonography

Ultrasound can be used in a completely different way to measure movement. When an object which emits, or reflects, waves is moving with constant velocity, a stationary observer will find that the frequency of the waves received is different depending on whether the object is moving towards or away from the observer. This is known as the **Doppler effect**. Doppler ultrasound devices measure the frequency shift in the ultrasound signal reflected from a moving object, the frequency shift being proportional to the velocity of the object along the axis of the beam. This effect can be used to study the rate of blood flow in veins and arteries, where the moving objects are red blood cells.

We need to derive a formula for calculating the change in frequency as follows. Let V be the speed of sound in air and v_s be the speed of the source of sound. If the transmitted frequency of the sound is f then we have two cases.

Source of sound moving towards the stationary observer

If the source of sound is stationary then the wavelength of the source of sound would be

$$\lambda = \frac{V}{f}$$

If the source is moving then, in one second, f waves will be emitted and the source will move a distance v_s. The distance occupied by the f waves will thus be $(V - v_s)$.

The wavelength λ' of the waves reaching the observer is given by:

$$\frac{V - v_s}{f}$$

The apparent frequency $f' = \dfrac{V}{\lambda'}$

Therefore $f' = \dfrac{V}{V - v_s} f$

Since $V - v_s$ is less than V, f' is is greater than f. The apparent frequency is increased. The change in frequency Δf is given by:

$$\Delta f = f' - f = f v_s / (V - v_s)$$

Source of sound moving away from the observer

In this case the expression becomes:

$$f' = \frac{V}{V + v_s} f$$

and the frequency change is:

$$\Delta f = f - f' = f v_s / (V + v_s)$$

(figure 5.10).

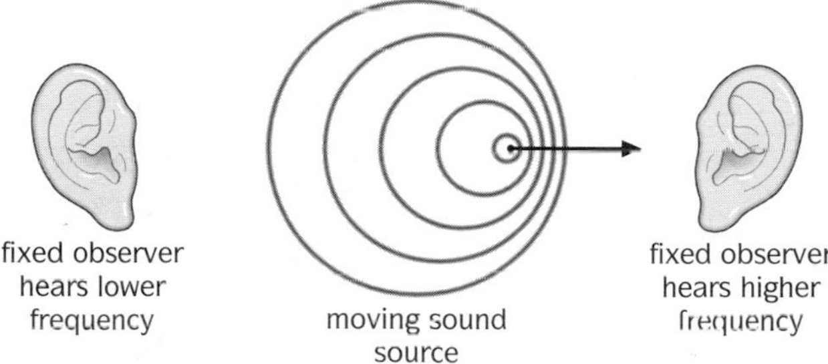

● ***Figure 5.10*** Change in frequency heard when source of sound is moving.

When used to monitor blood flow, there is a Doppler shift on both the outgoing and returning signals and so the total frequency shift is

$$\Delta f = 2fv/(V + v_s)$$

where v is the component of velocity of the red blood cells along the beam axis.

There are two types of Doppler system, continuous and pulsed. In the **continuous Doppler system**, a narrow beam of waves, of between 2 and 10 MHz, is transmitted by one transducer while a second transducer acts as a receiver. The Doppler signals are generated by mixing the transmitted and received signals. One of the main uses of this technique is to obtain information about the carotid artery, a major artery in the neck which carries blood to the brain. Arteries can be made narrower as a result of disease. This causes an increase in the rate of blood flow and in blood pressure which can damage small blood vessels. This is particularly dangerous in the brain. The carotid artery is near to the skin and so is easy to scan by this method.

A **pulsed Doppler system** gives range resolution, that is defining a small volume at a given depth from which the signal will be analysed. This is achieved by transmitting pulses of ultrasound and opening a receiver gate for a short period between pulses; the gate delay determines the maximum distance between the transducer and the reflecting surface. By using a large number of gates, in a multichannel flow detector, blood flow can be examined all along the beam. By scanning in a similar way to the B scan, a two-dimensional image of the velocity pattern can be obtained *(figure 5.11)*.

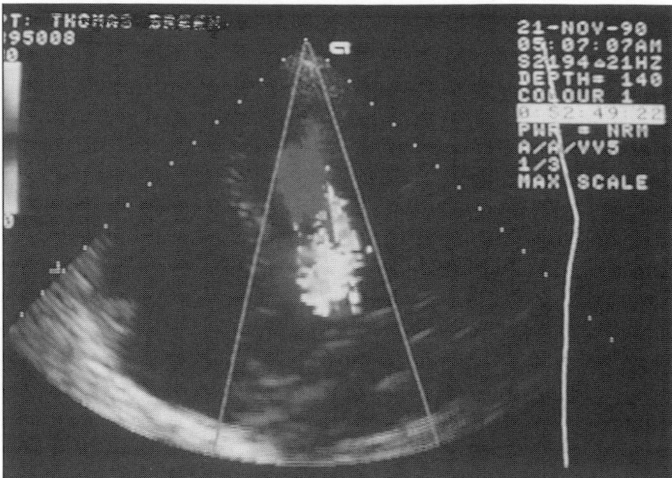

● ***Figure 5.11*** Doppler scan of blood flow through a heart valve.

Colour Doppler imaging

The technique of colour Doppler, or flow, imaging provides information as it happens (that is in real time). The Doppler shift at each point of the scan is colour coded and superimposed on the normal two-dimensional grey scale pictures which display the anatomical information from the B scan. The colours red, blue, yellow, cyan and white are used to indicate the direction and speed of flow: red indicates a positive flow (that is the blood is travelling towards the transducer) and blue indicates a negative flow (that is away from the transducer). Different shades of blue and red represent different speeds. This technique is very important in cardiac studies where it can be used to study abnormalities of blood flow within a damaged heart. It is particularly useful in the diagnosis of defects in the heart valves.

SAQ 5.3

a Describe what is meant by the Doppler effect when applied to sound.

b State the advantages of this technique when used in the imaging of organs using ultrasound.

Nuclear medicine in diagnosis

As described on page 39, nuclear medicine (the medical use of a radioactive chemical) can be used to produce images for diagnosis. The radionuclide used is usually technetium-99m and the images are generally produced with a gamma camera.

The gamma camera can be used in two different types of study:

- **static study** in which there is a time delay between injecting the radioactive material into the body and obtaining the images;
- **dynamic study** in which the amount of radiation in an organ is measured as a function of time by

taking a series of images, usually starting as the radioactive material is injected.

An example of a static study is where a patient is suffering from pulmonary embolism, that is a shortness of breath caused by a blood clot in the lungs. To obtain a scan the patient is injected with albumin suspended in saline and labelled with technetium-99m. The radioactive albumin is trapped in the fine capillaries of the lungs, so the scan will show how well the blood is distributed within the lungs. Any region to which blood flow has been prevented by the clot will show as blank parts of the lungs *(figure 5.12)*. The condition can be cured by administering certain drugs which dissolve the clots.

An example of a dynamic study is a renogram, which examines the function of the kidneys. In this case, a radioactive chemical is chosen which is normally extracted from the bloodstream by the kidneys within a few minutes. Ten to fifteen minutes after administration, most of the material should be in the bladder. The gamma camera is used to measure the radioactivity every 20–30 seconds for about 20 minutes, and the data sent to a computer. The computer will combine the data and produce a graph of activity against time.

SAQ 5.4

Look at the renogram in *figure 5.13* which shows the radioactivity in the left and right kidneys in a patient after the administration of a radiopharmaceutical. Which kidney is not functioning correctly, and what is the evidence for this?

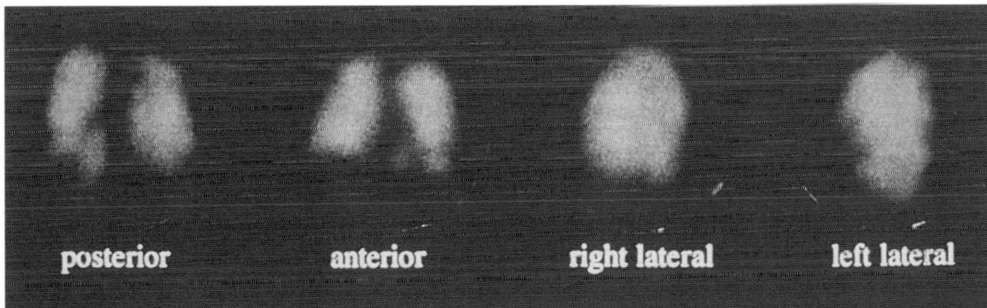

● ***Figure 5.12*** Scan of lungs after perfusion with radioactive albumin.

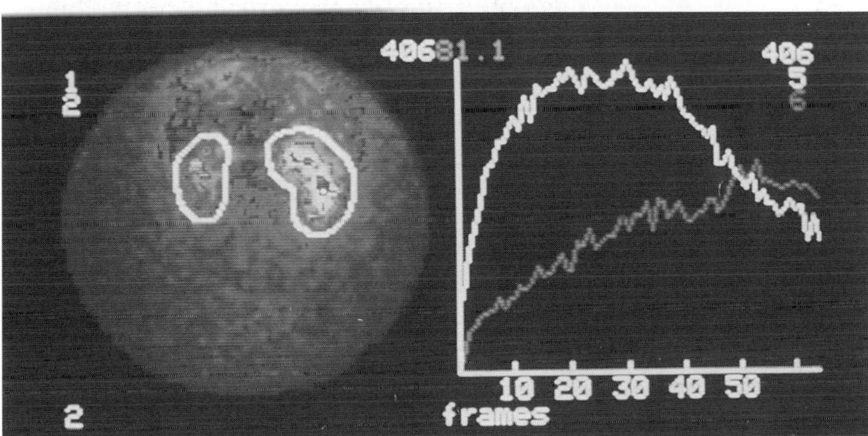

● ***Figure 5.13*** Renogram. The left hand picture shows a scan through the body and the kidneys at a point during the renogram study. The graph shows the radioactivity in the kidneys. The white line is the radioactivity in the right kidney, the grey line is the radioactivity in the left kidney.

Magnetic resonance imaging (MRI)

The technique of MRI was developed in 1946 as a method of studying atomic and molecular structure, but it was not until 1973 that it was suggested that MRI might be useful in medical imaging.

The principle behind MRI is that the nuclei in certain atoms and molecules behave as small magnets. Both protons and neutrons in the nucleus have properties of spin, and this spin may be in one of two directions. If there are even numbers of both protons and neutrons then there are equal numbers spinning in each direction and the effects cancel – we say that there is *no net spin*. However, if there is an odd number of either protons or neutrons then the spins cannot cancel. Nuclei which possess this net spin include hydrogen, phosphorus and carbon-13. The most important nucleus of these is hydrogen, which has only one proton and no neutrons, and is common in the body (particularly as a constituent of water). Nuclei with a net spin behave as small magnets, and have a magnetic 'north–south' axis.

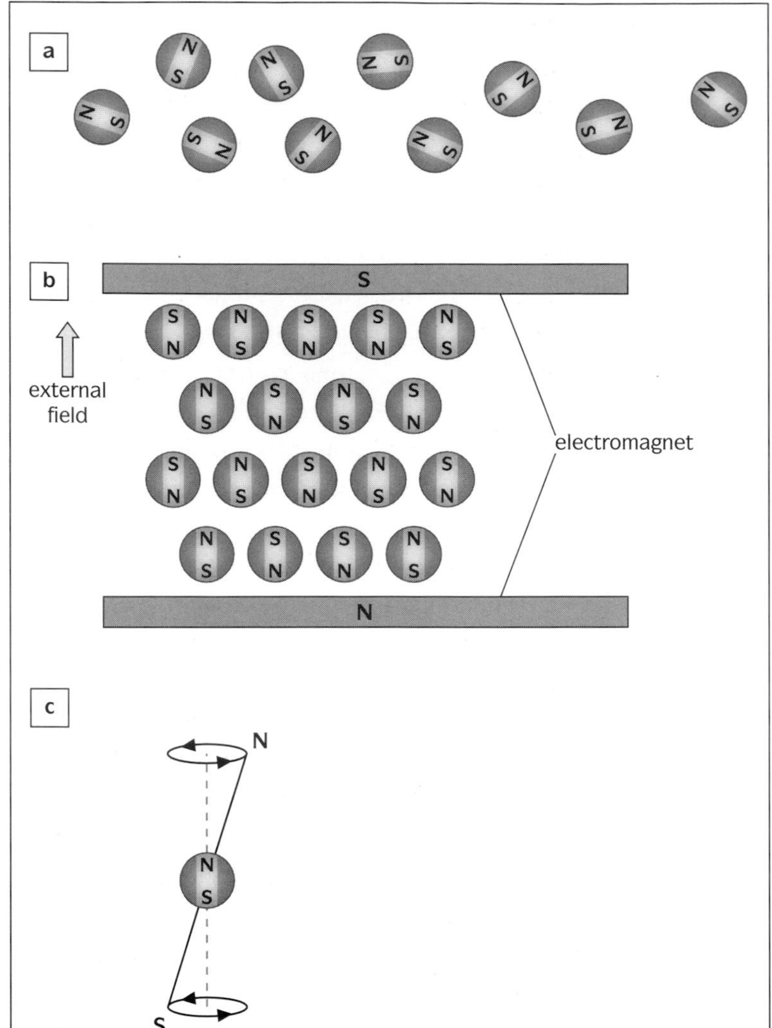

● ***Figure 5.14*** Diagrams representing the orientation of magnetic axes of nuclei before and after application of a strong, external magnetic field. **a** Normal alignment is random. **b** When a strong external magnetic field is applied, the nuclei are forced to align either in the same direction or in exactly the opposite direction to the field. **c** The magnetic axis of a nucleus precesses, just like that of a spinning top.

Normally the magnetic properties of hydrogen atoms are not detectable, since the magnetic axes of the nuclei are randomly aligned, and the net effect is zero in all directions *(figure 5.14a)*. If a strong magnetic field is applied, these nuclei will align themselves with the applied magnetic field. Unlike compass needles, which will all point in the same direction, the magnetic nuclei will align themselves either in the same direction as the field or in exactly the opposite direction *(figure 5.14b)*.

There is a very small preference for the same direction as the external field because the nuclei have slightly less energy in this position than if they point in the opposite direction. In a million nuclei, about four more will point in the direction of the field than will oppose it. The magnetic field due to the nuclei with net spin is very weak.

This nuclear magnetism would be impossible to detect in the presence of the external field if it remained pointing in the same direction all the time. However, the direction of the magnetic axis of a nucleus rotates around the direction of the external field, just as the axis of a spinning top rotates. This spinning is called **precessing** *(figure 5.14c)*. The frequency of this precessing (called the **Larmor frequency**) depends upon the composition of the nucleus and the strength of the external magnetic field. The Larmor frequency corresponds to a frequency in the radio frequency (RF) part of the electromagnetic spectrum.

The precessing nuclei aligned in the external magnetic field are subjected to pulses of RF radiation at the Larmor frequency. Resonance occurs, because the radio waves are 'in tune' with the precessing nuclei, and energy is transferred from the radio waves to the nuclei. This energy causes the direction of the magnetic axes to 'flip' by 90° or 180°. After each radio pulse ends, the nuclei return to their original, aligned state (they are said to **relax**) by two different electromagnetic processes, giving out an RF signal as they do so. This signal has an initial amplitude proportional to the number of nuclei present, and the amplitude decreases over time. The shape of the graph of amplitude against time can be analysed to give quantities known as **relaxation times** (there are two quantities, T_1 and T_2, one for each of the electromagnetic relaxation processes).

It is found that large differences occur in relaxation times between tissue containing hydrogen bound in water molecules and tissue containing hydrogen bound with other molecules. This means that tissues with different water content will show

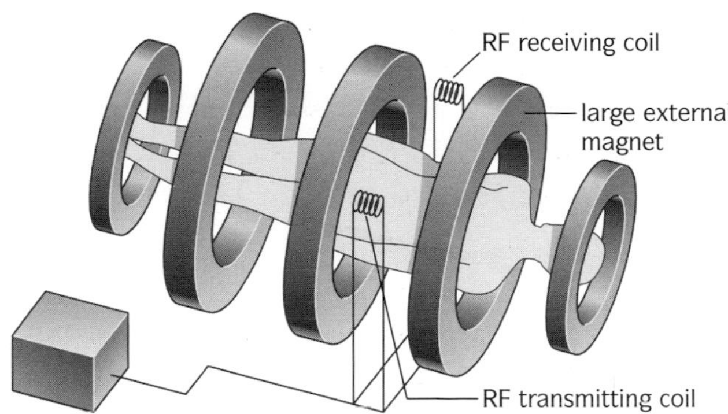

● ***Figure 5.15*** Arrangement of apparatus used in magnetic resonance imaging.

up on the scan. It is particularly useful for looking at cancerous tissues, which are active areas of growth with a high blood flow and therefore a high water content, because they show up clearly against the background tissue where growth is not so fast. Haemoglobin molecules in the blood also provide a resonance signal, so will produce a larger signal in areas of high blood flow.

MRI scans of the brain show more detail than X-ray images because the grey matter has more water-bound hydrogen (from a greater rate of blood flow through these areas) than the white matter.

The apparatus is shown in *figure 5.15*. There are five main features.

- A large electromagnet produces a large external magnetic field – superconducting magnets are now used because they produce large magnetic fields in a small space and at low running cost. The strength of this field can be varied from 0.1 to 2.0 tesla.
- A set of sweep (gradient) coils produce a magnetic field that varies in strength over a small range.
- A radio frequency oscillator emits radiation at a certain frequency.
- A radio receiver which detects the frequency of radiation given out as the nuclei come back into alignment.
- A computer which controls the gradient coils and radio frequency pulses, storing and analysing the received signals. It also reconstructs the data into images and displays them.

Procedure in MRI

The patient is placed in the strong magnetic field where it is most intense, that is in the centre of the field for an electromagnet. The small sweep coils then vary the magnetic field strength across the patient's body so that there is a known, unique field strength value at each point within the patient and therefore a unique value for the frequency of oscillation of the hydrogen atoms at each point. A pulse of radio waves is then applied to the body to flip the magnetic axes of the nuclei. This causes a signal to be generated that is proportional to the number of hydrogen atoms at that point. By changing the frequency of the radio waves slightly, resonance will occur at a different point where the magnetic field is correct for the new frequency. It is then possible to build up a picture of the hydrogen concentration throughout the body.

An image of the hydrogen concentration is relatively trivial compared to the information that can be obtained by measuring the relaxation times. If the hydrogen atoms are in a solid structure, such as bone, the energy is lost so quickly that there is not sufficient time to measure any signal. This means that there is no MRI image of bone since it just appears as a blank space.

It is possible to do one measurement on a large number of points and then do a second measurement on all, then a third. At the end of an examination, the computer stores the information from all the signals from all points within a large volume of the body.

More data can be collected after introducing substances to the body which concentrate in particular organs and give an enhanced signal during the imaging process, thus highlighting these particular organs in the image in manner similar to that of X-ray contrast agents.

There are several advantages in using MRI.

- The most important advantage is that the method does not use ionising radiation which, even in small doses, will create a radiation hazard both to the patient and the staff.
- MRI gives better soft tissue contrast than computed tomography and generates data from a 3-D volume simultaneously.

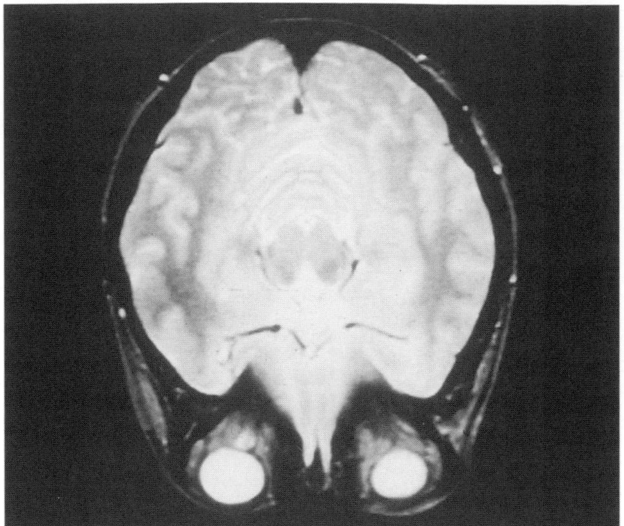

● ***Figure 5.16*** Magnetic resonance image of the brain.

■ The information in the computer can be displayed on a screen as a slice or a section in any direction or produce a simulated 3-D image *(figure 5.16)*.

■ There are no moving mechanisms involved in MRI; it just uses changing currents and magnetic fields.

■ There is no sensation, after-effects or side-effects at the field strengths used for routine diagnostic imaging. A relaxed patient can even sleep during the examination, although there is noise generated from the switching of the gradient coils.

There are some disadvantages. For example, metallic objects can be heated, and cardiac pacemakers can be upset since most are designed to be altered by applying magnetic or radio fields. One hazard is that loose steel objects could be drawn into the magnet. The room must also be screened from external radio fields.

SAQ 5.5

Suggest why MRI would be used in preference to CT scans.

Light in diagnosis

Light can be used for both diagnosis and treatment. Here we will look at diagnosis, its use in treatment is dealt with in chapter 6. There are several uses of light in diagnosis but two important examples are pulse oximetry and endoscopy.

Pulse oximetry

This technique uses light to measure the oxygen saturation level of the blood in tissues and also to measure the pulse rate. Both measurements can be calculated from the absorption of selected wavelengths of light.

Light is produced in a probe (usually by a light-emitting diode) and passed through the tissue. Some light is absorbed by the tissue and the light that passes through is received by a photodetector in an oximeter which converts the intensity of the light into an electrical signal. The circuitry in the oximeter converts the intensity measurements into measures of oxygen saturation level and pulse rates.

The oximeter operates on the assumption that haemoglobin, the oxygen-carrying molecule in the blood, exists in two forms:

■ an oxygenated form in which the oxygen molecules are loosely bound to the haemoglobin;

■ a reduced form with no bound oxygen molecules.

Different amounts of light are absorbed by these two forms of haemoglobin *(figure 5.17)*. The oximeter measures the relative absorption of red light at 660 nm and infrared light at 940 nm so

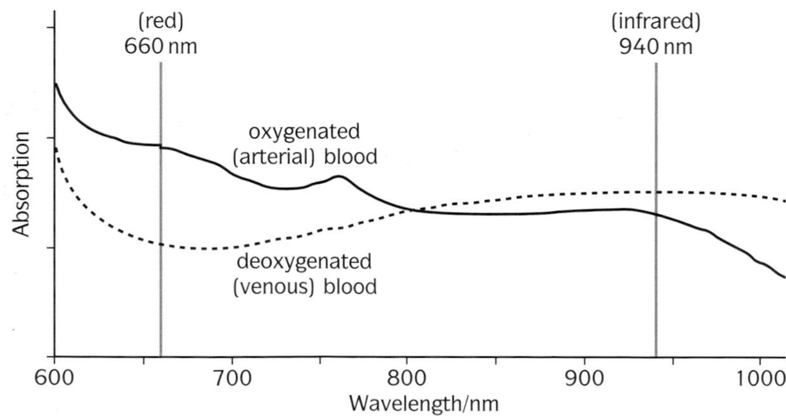

● ***Figure 5.17*** Absorption of light by oxygenated and deoxygenated (reduced) haemoglobin.

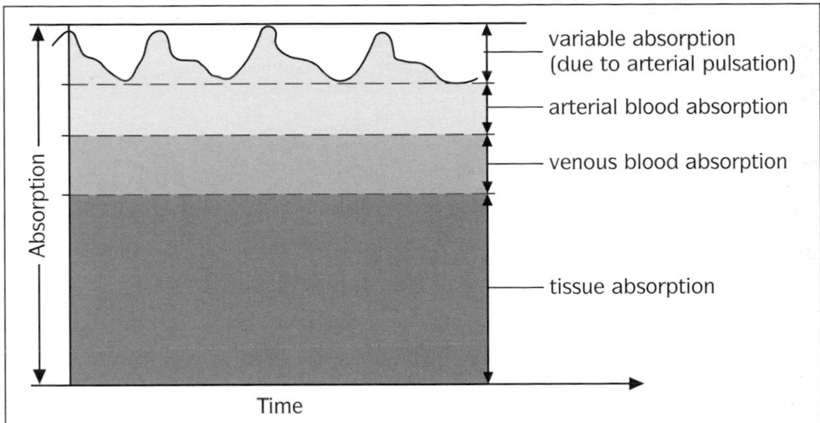

● ***Figure 5.18*** Absorption of light by tissue, arterial and venous blood.

that arterial and venous blood can be distinguished. The pulse rate can be measured in arteries because pulsation of the blood flow modulates the light passing through the tissue. Non-pulsing venous blood and tissues do not modulate the light but have a fixed value of absorption *(figure 5.18)*.

The probe consists of a red LED and an infrared LED together with a photodetector. These are combined as one complete probe which can be connected to an ear, a finger or a toe. They are used during operations so that the anaesthetist can continuously measure the quantities of oxygen content and pulse rate automatically. The oximeter displays this information visually and has audible alarms which signal any rapid change in the patient's condition. The oximeter can be also be used with premature babies to monitor continuously the oxygen content of their blood. Another application is in monitoring the blood oxygen content and pulse rate in cardiac patients to check the condition of the heart during exercise.

SAQ 5.6

Why would an LED be used in pulse oximetry rather than an ordinary light?

Endoscopes

Endoscopes use fibre optics to send a light along a tube and return an image so that it is possible to view inside the body. Endoscopes can be used along the tubes of the body, such as the trachea into the lungs, the oesophagus into the stomach and intestines, and into the bladder and bowels. They can also be inserted through a small incision to view internal parts of the body without the need for major surgery. The main advantage of using an endoscope is that it is a cold light source, so there is no heat delivered inside the body.

Two different arrangements of fibres are used, called coherent and incoherent. If the fibres are arranged so that they have exactly the same relative positions at each end of the bundle then an image can be built up at the other end of the bundle from the object. These are called **coherent**

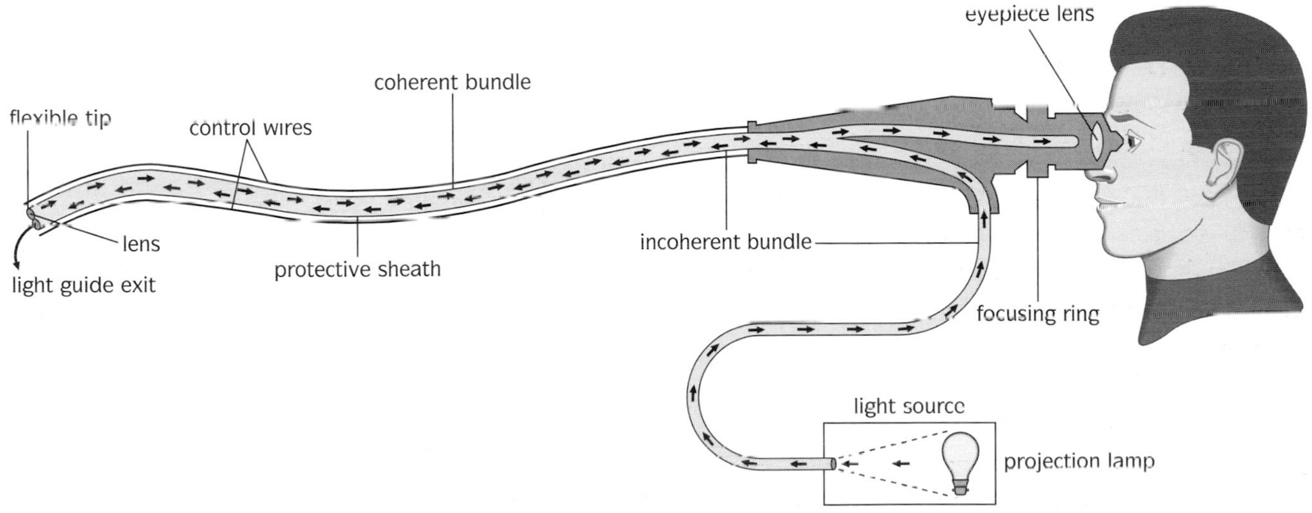

● ***Figure 5.19*** Structure of an endoscope.

bundles. If the fibres are arranged in a random way then the bundle is **incoherent**. Incoherent fibre bundles are cheaper to produce. In both cases, the ends of the bundle are evenly cut and polished.

The endoscope is shown in *figure 5.19* and consists of four parts:

- an incoherent bundle which is used to send light down the tube;
- a coherent bundle which has a lens at the bottom end and is used to send reflected light back up the tube so that an image can be created;
- a channel for water which is used to clean the lens;
- another channel which allows liquids to be taken out of the body or biopsy probes to be put into the body to obtain very small tissue samples from inside the body.

The tube is round and reasonably flexible. The far end is more flexible and can be moved around by the operator by means of control wires.

Almost all wavelengths of laser light can be passed along the endoscope except those that are in the infrared region, because quartz in the fibres absorbs these wavelengths.

SAQ 5.7

a What are the advantages in using an endoscope to see inside the body?

b Fibre optics work on the principle of total internal reflection. Describe this principle and explain why different types of fibres will affect the final image.

SUMMARY

- Non-invasive techniques are useful since they do not involve surgery and allow parts of the body to be imaged.
- Ultrasound waves are waves beyond the range of human hearing. They are generated by a piezoelectric transducer.

  Ultrasound is particularly useful in looking at unborn babies and examining soft tissue. It will not show bones or gas-filled structures. This is because most of the ultrasound is reflected at these structures and very little is transmitted.

  Doppler ultrasound is used to measure flow rates of fluids within the body.
- Magnetic resonance imaging is used to obtain images of organs of the body without using ionising radiation. When the patient is placed in a magnetic field and a pulse of radiation applied, then certain frequencies may be detected.
- The pulse oximeter calculates the oxygen content of blood and pulse rate by measuring the absorption of light as it passes through blood vessels in tissue.
- Endoscopes can be used to view inside the body with little or no surgery. Nearly all sources of light can be used and they have the advantage that they are a cold light source.

Questions

1 Imaging of the human body represents a major proportion of the work of a medical physicist. Describe the major features of this technique and describe one method in detail.

2 Magnetic resonance imaging has been described as a major safe advance in the imaging of the human body.
  a What are the key features in the process and why is it a safe method?
  b Describe the key parts of the machine that allow such an image to be taken.

3 What methods would you use to produce an image for the investigation of the following? Explain your reasons and describe the limitations of your choice.
  a Brain
  b Blood flow in the heart
  c Development of a fetus
  d Stomach ulcer

Medical treatment

By the end of this chapter you should be able to:

1 describe the use of X-rays in the treatment of cancers;
2 describe the use of implanted radioactive sources in the treatment of cancer;
3 describe a variety of uses of lasers in medical treatment;
4 describe the uses of ultrasound in therapy;
5 describe photochemotherapy.

Radiotherapy is a branch of medical treatment which uses radioactive materials as medicines. The main use of radiotherapy is to kill off cancerous cells while sparing normal tissue. During treatment the affected parts of the body might be given large radiation doses, divided into smaller, regular amounts and delivered over a period of several weeks. The treatment may use external beams of radiation (usually X-rays but also electrons), or the implantation of radioactive sources or the administration of unsealed radionuclides.

Use of external X-ray sources in treating malignancies

During the treatment of malignancies, both when using X-rays and radioactive sources, it is important that the cancerous cells are killed while the normal tissue is spared. Rather than give a single large dose of radiation, the radiation is split into a number of small doses called **fractions** which are given over a period of time. This fractionation technique has two advantages.

- Cells are more sensitive to radiation when they are dividing, but may spend more time in a state where they are not dividing. Cells that were not sensitive during one dose may be radiosensitive during another and so will be killed. Cancerous cells divide more rapidly than normal cells and so are more likely to be radiosensitive during treatment.
- Normal cells recover more rapidly between fractions, and so a higher total radiation dose can be tolerated by the patient.

It is useful to define the term **target volume**, which is the volume of tissue within the patient that is to be irradiated to a given absorbed dose in a certain time. The energy given to the target volume must be significantly higher than that given to the surrounding healthy tissue if dangerous side-effects are to be avoided. This is particularly true if surrounding areas include radiosensitive tissues and organs such as the spinal cord, kidneys and the lens of the eye.

Treatment planning

To achieve the best results from radiotherapy, the distribution of the radiation, called the **dose distribution**, must be calculated accurately. The use of computers can make this calculation easier. First the doctor needs information about the position and size of the tumour volume. This is obtained from X-ray or MRI images of the target volume from different angles. MRI scanners are particularly useful for soft tissue tumours. These images are recorded either on film or an image intensifier and transferred to the treatment planning computer. From this the doctor tries to find the best geometric arrangement of radiation fields to give an acceptable dose distribution around the patient.

The data can be used to plot isodose curves which are lines joining points of equal percentage dose. In *figure 6.1a* the isodose curves for an unmodified beam are shown. However, the shape of the curves can be altered using a thin lead wedge which is placed in the treatment beam. These wedges alter the intensity of the beam across the field because they are of non-uniform shape, as shown in *figure 6.1b*. Similar effects can be obtained by using shaped blocks, known as **compensators**, which are positioned over the patient.

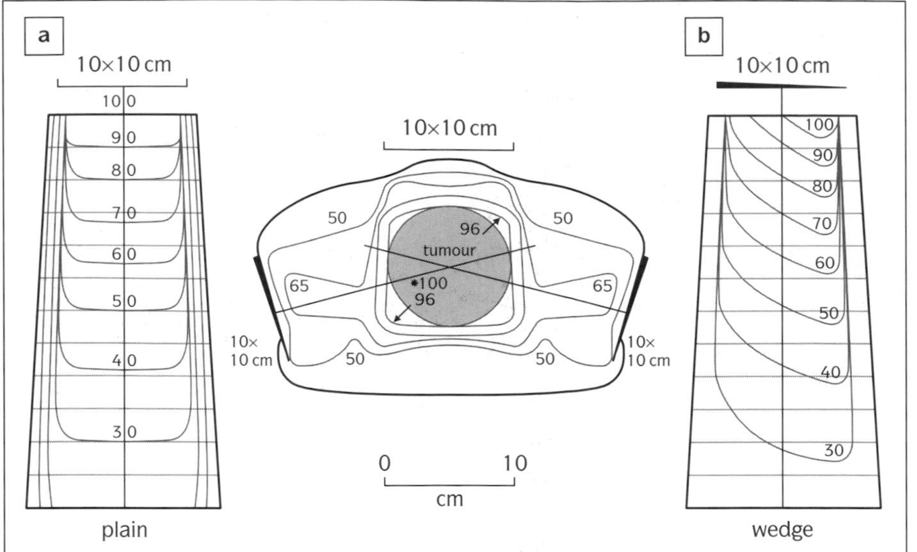

● ***Figure 6.1*** Treatment plan for irradiating a tumour with X-rays. The isodose curves on the left are without the wedge; those on the right show how a thin lead wedge affects the isodose curves.

The isodose curves are measured in a water tank and assume that the patient is perpendicular to the beam, that body tissue is homogeneous and has the same attenuation properties as water. The presence of tissues with different properties, particularly air cavities such as the lungs, can greatly alter the dose distribution. The curvature of the body surface will also make the isodose curves asymmetric.

The treatment planning computer works out the dose distribution resulting from irradiating the patient from different angles; the dose delivered by each beam may be different. Wedges are used to compensate for body curvature, to 'trim' the beam near a critical organ, or to ensure dose uniformity within the target volume when the beams are not spaced equally around the patient. Several treatment schedules will be calculated and the best one, which gives the necessary dose to the target volume while minimising damage to normal tissue, will be selected for use. A final treatment plan is shown in *figure 6.2* for a patient suffering from carcinoma of the brain.

In order to check the accuracy of the treatment plan prior to treatment, the patient will be examined in a simulator. This machine has a rotating gantry similar to the treatment machine, but is fitted with a diagnostic X-ray system and an image intensifier. The system produces a film of the area to be treated, with markers showing the edges of the treatment field as calculated in the treatment plan. Test X-ray images are obtained to check that the target volume will be irradiated as planned.

SAQ 6.1

Why is it useful to use a dose treatment plan and what is meant by isodose curves?

External beam therapy

The normal radiation source used in this treatment is a **linear accelerator**, which produces X-rays by accelerating electrons to a high velocity using a radio frequency wave. The high energy electron beam is deflected by a magnet and focused onto a target in which the X-rays are produced (*figure 6.3*). The conversion to X-rays is more efficient at these large energies (4–20 MeV) than at the voltages used for ordinary diagnostic X-rays.

The X-ray beam is trimmed to the desired shape by moveable shutters in a collimator. The positioning of the beam can be checked prior to treatment by using a light source which is arranged to

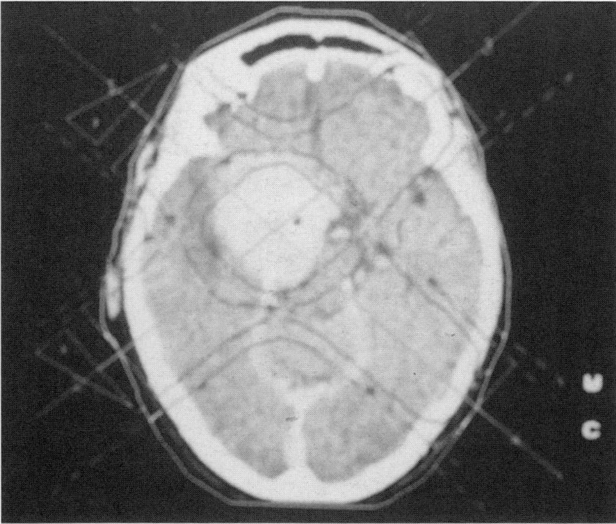

● ***Figure 6.2*** Final treatment plan for patient suffering carcinoma of the brain.

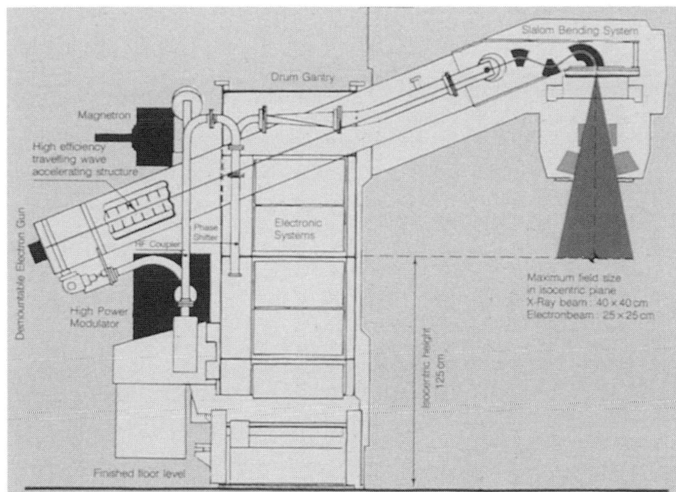

● ***Figure 6.3*** Linear accelerator.

simulate the beam exactly. The whole accelerator, target and collimator is mounted to rotate about the treatment couch, and can move in all three dimensions *(figure 6.4)*.

Gamma rays from a cobalt teletherapy unit can be used instead of X-ray treatment for some types of cancer. The radiation source is a pellet of cobalt-60. This emits high energy gamma radiation with a half-life of 5.3 years. Unlike the linear accelerator, the radiation cannot be switched off, so the cobalt pellet has to be stored in a totally shielded position. It is moved mechanically from the storage position to the treatment position in a shielded sphere that has an aperture from which the treatment beam emerges. The edges of the treatment beam are less well-defined than for the linear accelerator because of the relatively large size of the radioactive source. This makes it more difficult to achieve a sharp fall-off in radiation dose at the edges of the target volume. So these machines tend to be used where this problem is not so important, as in total body irradiation.

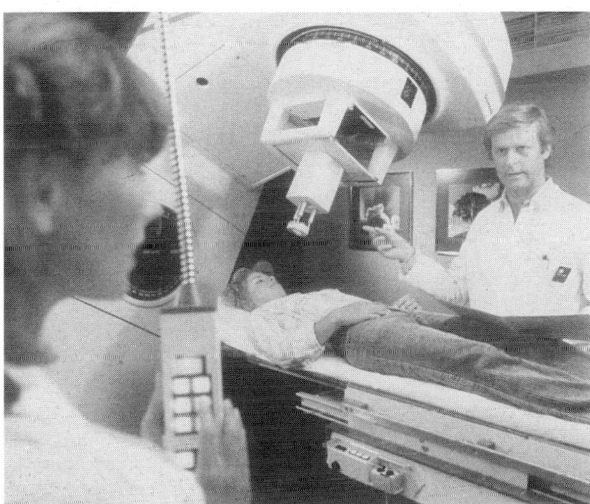

● ***Figure 6.4*** Accelerator, target and collimator mounted to move around treatment couch.

In both X-ray and gamma ray treatment, the patient is positioned so that the tumour volume is sited at the centre of rotation and the machine rotates about the patient from one treatment position to another. To ensure correct positioning a laser beam alignment system is used. This uses a low-powered helium–neon laser.

SAQ 6.2

Many hospitals have replaced their cobalt sources with linear accelerators. Suggest why this change has been made.

If the target in the linear accelerator is moved out of the beam path, an electron beam is generated. This can be used to treat tumours which are at shallow depths, for example certain skin tumours. Since the tumour is superficial the electron beam is placed directly over the tumour.

There are problems with external beam therapy: for example large volumes of tissue are irradiated, including tissue between the body surface and the tumour. Shielding by bone can also be a problem. Some of these problems can be overcome by using implant or radionuclide therapy.

Surface and implant therapy

Since the beginning of the twentieth century when Pierre and Marie Curie first prepared a sample of radium-226, small radioactive sources in many shapes and sizes have been used in radiotherapy. Metal tubes and needles packed with radium-226 or caesium-137 have been particularly popular, and in recent years, iridium-191 has been introduced. Plaques and shaped eye applicators containing cobalt-60, strontium-90 and ruthenium-106 are also available *(figure 6.5)*.

The disadvantage of using this kind of therapy is that the dose patterns are very uneven. Underdoses

● ***Figure 6.5*** Applicators for surface and/or implant radiotherapy.

of radiation can be avoided only by allowing some regions of overdose. These are of small dimensions and are tolerable and repairable.

These kinds of sources can be used in three different ways.

- **Surface applicators** are arrays of sources placed near to or in contact with the patient's skin for superficial treatments. They are used in treating the eye.
- **Interstitial implants** use radioactive wire or arrays of needle-like radioactive sources implanted directly into the target volume. They can be used for breast cancer.
- With **intracavitary methods**, the sources are sealed into special containers and inserted into the appropriate body cavity. These are frequently used for the treatment of cancer of the cervix.

These sources are shown in *figure* 6.6.

Interstitial and intracavitary treatments generally take a few days during which the sources remain in the patient. It is now possible to have high dose rate 'after loading' techniques which significantly reduce treatment times. These methods involve the insertion of tubes, or hollow applicators attached to tubes, into the organ or tissues to be treated. During the operation no radioactive sources are

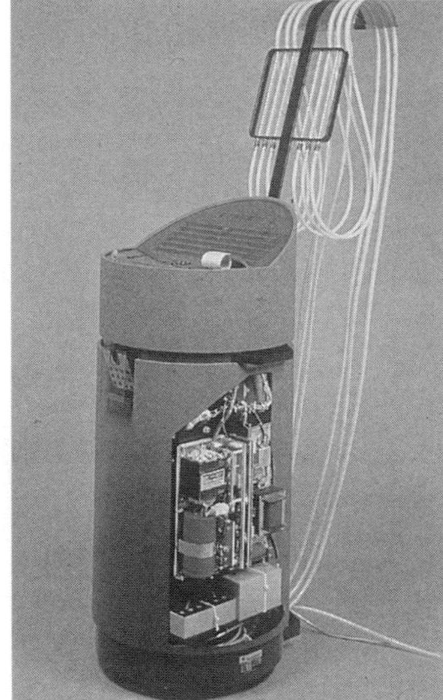

● ***Figure 6.6*** Sealed sources.

present. After the tubes are correctly positioned they are connected to the source storage device and the sources are blown into position using compressed air. This often occurs after the patient has been transferred to a specially protected room. With many of these treatments, the final distribution of radioactive sources in the patient is not exactly the same as the planned, idealised distribution and radiographic checks are necessary.

Radionuclide therapy

Alpha and beta emissions, together with low energy X- and gamma photons, are classed as 'non-penetrating' radiations. This means that they are wholly absorbed within the patient's body and so are not useful in diagnostic imaging, since they only increase the radiation dose to the patient without making it possible to produce an image. However, they can be useful in therapy.

If the radioactive material can be deposited at the site of the cancer, the radiation will destroy the surrounding abnormal tissue while sparing more distant normal tissue. This kind of radiotherapy can only be used in those cases in which a suitable chemical can be used to carry the radionuclide to the site of the tumour.

A common example of this kind of radiotherapy is the treatment of an overactive thyroid (known as thyrotoxicosis) which was first used in 1948. The thyroid gland requires iodine to produce the hormone thyroxine. Iodine is only found in minute amounts in the rest of the body, so radioactive iodine introduced into the body will mostly collect in the thyroid. This is known as **targetting**. The radioactive iodine is used in either liquid or capsule form.

The amount of radioactivity of ^{131}I to be administered is usually based on a simple calculation according to the size of the gland. There are certain restrictions which patients must observe because of the risk of irradiating other people. For example, journeys on public transport should be limited to one hour and patients should stay at home until the level of radioactivity has dropped to a safe level.

SAQ 6.3

When radioactive sources are placed inside the body, the distribution of radiation is not always as planned. Explain why this method of treatment will not always be satisfactory.

Ultrasound in therapy

Though ultrasound is most commonly used in imaging and diagnosis, as described in chapter 5, high power ultrasound can also be used for therapeutic purposes. In physiotherapy departments, ultrasound is used to heat injured muscle tissue, causing increased blood flow to accelerate the rate of healing. Another use is in the breaking up of kidney stones using a device known as a lithotripter. Very high powered waves from two or more transducers are sent in to the patient through gauze pads impregnated with coupling jelly. The patient is positioned so that the beams focus at the position of the kidney stone. The high intensity generated at this focus causes shock waves which fragment the stones into small particles. These can then be passed out through the urine.

Lasers

Lasers have two particular features which make them useful in medical treatment:

- the radiation produced is all of the same wavelength; in contrast, an ordinary white light source, even when passed through a coloured filter, will still contain a mixture of wavelengths;
- the power density of cross-section of the beam is very large compared to a normal white light source. The light over the whole diameter of the exit beam is in phase and can be focused to a spot, achieving very high power densities.

It is the power density, rather than the total power, which allows the beam to cut through materials. While the output of a typical school helium–neon laser is perhaps 0.1 mW, the beam diameter is typically 3 mm at a distance of 2 m. This gives a power density of $14\,\mathrm{W\,m^{-2}}$. For a 100 W lamp at the same distance, the energy is spread over a sphere of surface area $4\pi r^2$. As the lamp can be taken to be only 10% efficient in its conversion of electrical energy to light, this gives an intensity of $0.2\,\mathrm{W\,m^{-2}}$. This means that particular care should be taken to avoid laser light entering the eye, even though the power output is very small.

The output from a laser can be pulsed or continuous, depending on the type of treatment to be given. *Table 6.1* gives the details of different lasers used in medicine. The data shown are for continuous power outputs unless otherwise stated.

Type of laser	*Wavelength/nm*	*Typical power*
argon	488 or 514	0.5–1 W
dye	550–700 (dependent on dye)	100–500 mW
helium–neon	633	1–5 mW
gallium arsenide	910	1 mW
neodymium YAG	1064	25–50 W 50 kW (pulsed) 1 MW
carbon dioxide	10 600	15–20 W
excimer	193	20 W

● ***Table 6.1***

SAQ 6.4

Describe **two** features of a laser that make it useful in medical treatments.

Lasers are used in medical treatment in a variety of ways. Three common treatments are described below.

- **Using the laser as a scalpel**
  When surgeons cut through tissue with a scalpel they also cut through minor blood vessels. These bleed into the working area and make it more difficult to see what is being operated on. A carbon dioxide laser can be used to allow bloodless surgery. As the laser cuts through the tissue heat from the beam will cause the tissue (including the small blood vessels) to shrink and harden. Water in the tissue will be vapourised. There will be a very slight charring at the edges of the blood vessels but this is difficult to see.
- **Removal of birthmarks and tattoos**
  A common birthmark is a port wine coloured stain on the skin which is caused by abnormal growth of blood vessels beneath the skin. An argon laser, which produces a blue-green light, can be used to reduce the effect. The light will be absorbed by the dark blood vessels and will seal them *(figure 6.7)*. This usually leaves a slight scar. Certain tattoos can also be partially removed. In this case, the laser energy is absorbed by the dye molecules used in the tattoo, causing them to break up.
- **Using a laser with an endoscope**
  A neodymium YAG laser can be used with an endoscope to destroy cancers which block a patient's airway. The treatment will not cure the patient but will make them more comfortable. Recently this laser has been used to vaporise blood clots and other deposits in veins and arteries. This required the development of small diameter, very flexible fibre optics which can be threaded into the patient's blood vessels. At present, success has been obtained in treating blood clots in the leg. In the future the technique may be extended to unblocking the arteries in the heart.

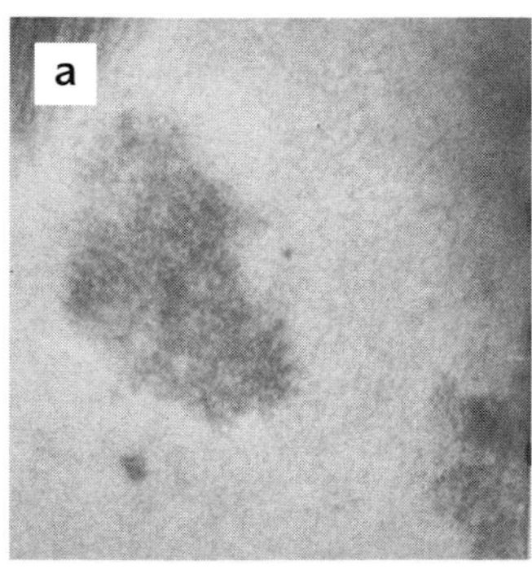

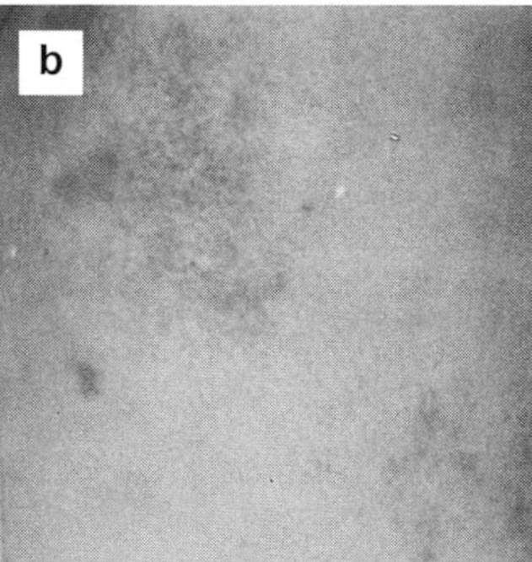

● ***Figure 6.7*** A birthmark
a before laser treatment
b after laser treatment.

Eye problems

Lasers can also be used to treat a variety of different eye problems.

- **Detached retina**
  Sometimes the retina can detach itself from the rear of the eyeball. It can be welded back into place using a pulsed ruby or argon laser. The laser is focused onto a particular spot, melting the tissue and forming a weld. A series of welds is used to re-attach the retina completely.
- **Diabetic retinopathy**
  Some people who suffer from diabetes experience a progressive deterioration of their vision. This happens because a network of new and 'leaky' blood vessels gradually develops in the retina from the edge inwards. Since blood is opaque, vision is lost. An argon laser can be used to seal the vessels, since the dark blood vessels absorb the light and change it to heat which causes the sealing. The treated area of the retina is destroyed, but further proliferation of the blood vessels is prevented so that the rest of the patient's sight will not be affected *(figure 6.8)*.
- **Strands of tissue**
  Cataracts are a developing opacity of the lens. This can be corrected by removing the natural lens and replacing it with a plastic lens (page 14). However, strands of opaque tissue can grow behind the new lens as the body's defence mechanisms recognise the new lens as a foreign body. A pulsed neodymium-YAG laser can be used to split the strands of tissue without damaging the lens. The correction to the patient's sight will be immediate.

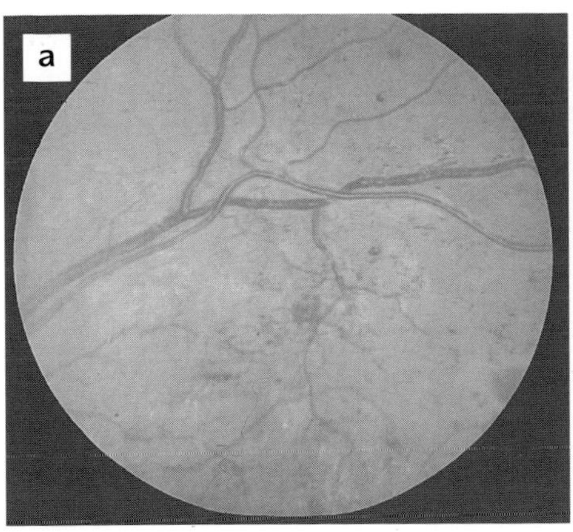

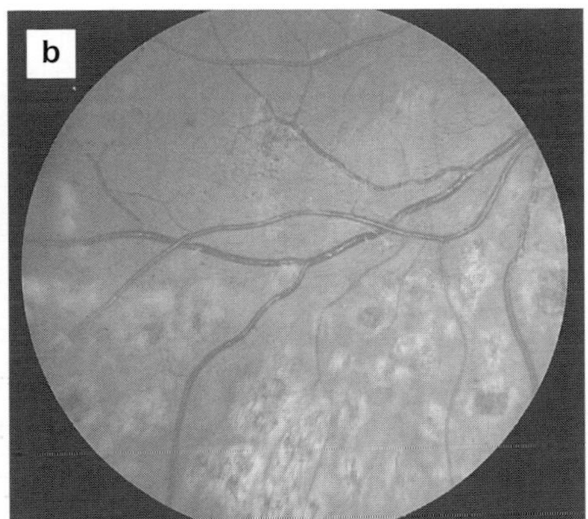

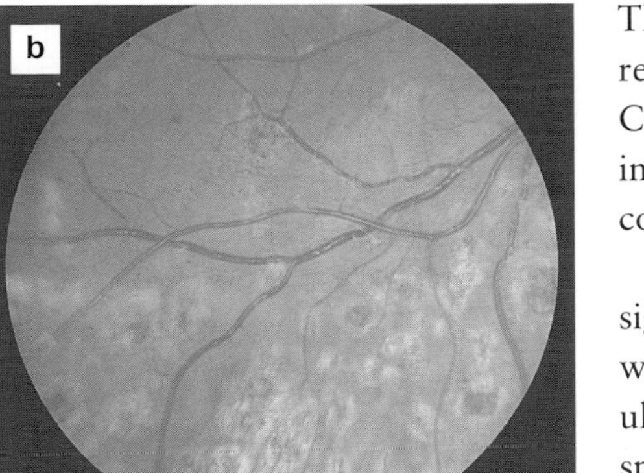

● ***Figure 6.8*** Retina

a before laser treatment for diabetic retinopathy

b after treatment.

SAQ 6.5

The visible spectrum ranges from 400–700 nm.

a Using *table 6.1*, decide which lasers operate in the infrared region of the spectrum.

b A laser has a power ouput of 20 W. Calculate the time required to dissipate 150 J of energy.

■ Correction of eye defects

A relatively recent technique using a laser allows a permanent correction to the eye defects described in chapter 2. This uses an excimer laser to produce incisions in the corneal surface.

The laser can also be used to reprofile the corneal surface. Care must be taken not to impair the transparency of the cornea.

In the correction of short sight (myopia), the laser light, which is transmitted in the ultraviolet region of the spectrum, is delivered through a set of apertures *(figure 6.9a)*. The apertures decrease in diameter as the wheel rotates. This allows more of the central area of the cornea to be removed than the edge. The length of time that each of the apertures remains open is controlled by a computer. The treatment uses a series of lenses and control systems that allow the light to be correctly focused onto the required part of the eye. The reprofiling of the cornea is shown in *figure 6.10a*.

A different set of apertures is used in the correction of long sight. The purpose is to remove more of the tissue at the edge of the cornea than at the centre. This is done by progressively larger openings which steepen the curvature of the cornea. The aperture wheel is shown in *figure 6.9b* and the effect on the cornea in *figure 6.10b*.

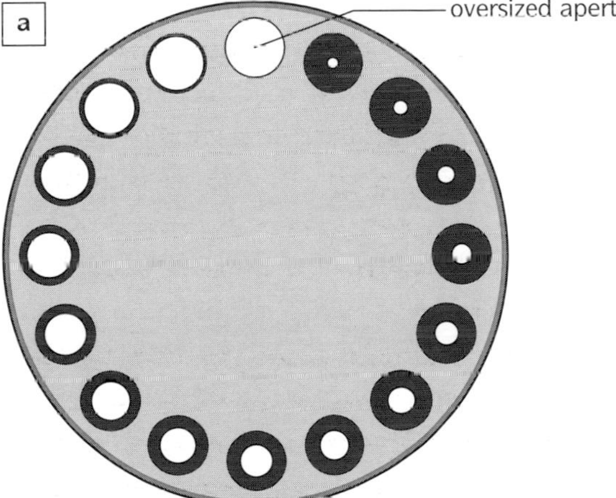

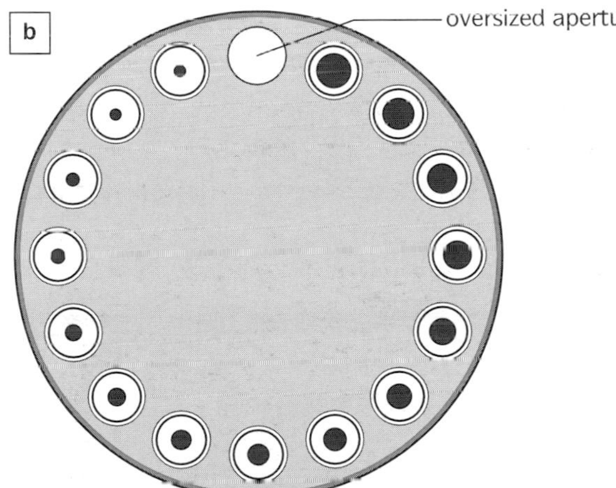

● ***Figure 6.9*** Aperture wheels for use with excimer laser to correct eye defects.

a Aperture wheel used for correcting myopia. The apertures let more light through the centre than the edge of each circle, so that more of the cornea is removed in the centre.

b Aperture wheel for correcting hypermetropia. The central disc in each aperture shields the centre of the cornea so more is removed from the edge.

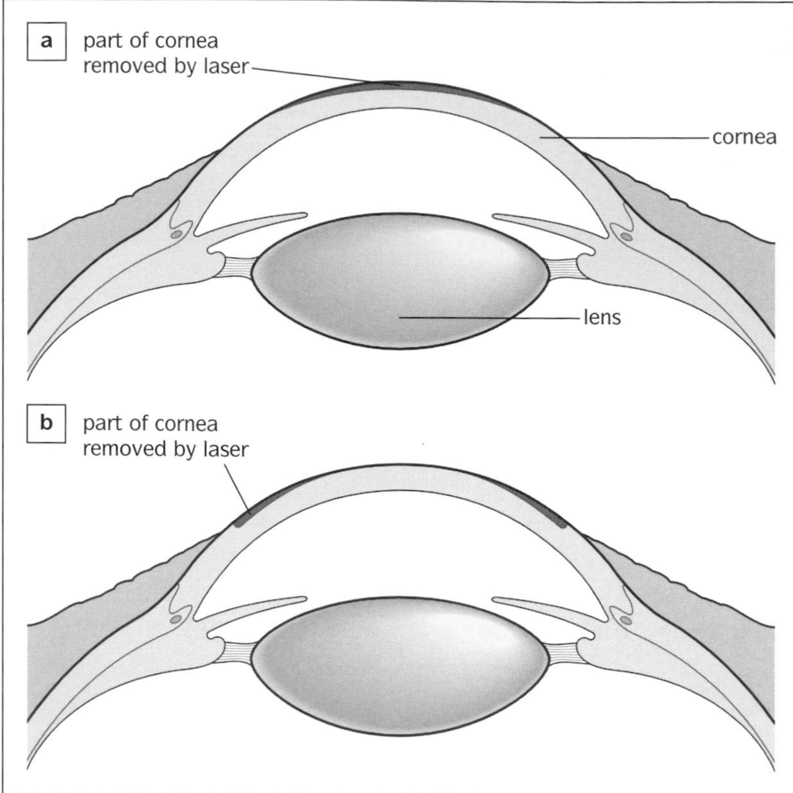

● *Figure 6.10* Diagrammatic representation of sections through the eye after treatment of the cornea by laser.
a Correction for myopia – the outer surface of the cornea is made flatter.
b Correction for hypermetropia – the outer surface of the cornea is made steeper.

Astigmatism may also be corrected using a series of rectangles which can be aligned and then rotated.

The application of the excimer laser for this type of treatment has only recently been developed. It is not successful in every case and has been found to create other defects or produce scarring of tissue in some cases.

Photochemotherapy

Another portion of the electromagnetic spectrum, ultraviolet (UV) light, can also be used in medical treatment, particularly for the skin condition psoriasis. In this case, the portion of the UV spectrum from 320 to 380 nm, known as UVA, is used in conjunction with the drug psoralen. Psoralen is taken up preferentially by the diseased cells and is activated by exposure to UVA radiation. It combines with the DNA in the cell and inhibits cell replication. Normal skin cells do not take up psoralen and so are unaffected by the radiation, other than a sunburn-like reddening. Before treatment is carried out, a quantity called the **minimum phototoxicity dose** (MPD) is first determined. This is the dose of UVA which just causes reddening of the skin. After this, the patient swallows the drug and irradiation takes place about 2 hours later, the initial dose of UVA used being the MPD. Patients may be treated as often as daily until the condition is cleared, and the dose of radiation can be increased as required.

SUMMARY

- An external beam of X-rays can be used as a method of treating cancer. This uses high energy X-rays.
- Radioactive sources can be implanted to treat certain types of cancerous tumours. This involves the insertion of containers into the patient to which the radioactive material is added.
- Radionuclides can be used to treat conditions of organs in which the nuclide can be targetted, as in the treatment of an overactive thyroid with radioactive iodine.
- Ultrasound can be used in therapy, to cause the break up of kidney stones.
- Lasers have a number of uses in medicine: as a scalpel, to seal blood vessels in the eye due to diabetes, to correct a detached retina, with an endoscope to break up cancerous tissue in airways and deposits inside blood vessels, and to correct some eye defects.
- UV light can be used with the drug psoralen to treat the skin condition psoriasis.

Questions

1 What are the main steps in treatment planning prior to the use of radiation in therapy?

2 Lasers are used in a wide range of treatments. Describe one of these uses in detail and state why the use of a laser is necessary in this case.

3 Ionising radiations are used to treat a wide range of cancers. Describe typical cases which may be treated by external and internal sources of radiation.

Working with radiation

By the end of this chapter you should be able to:

1 describe the structure of a film badge;

2 explain the correct use of the film badge;

3 explain how both the type of radiation and the total dose of radiation can be determined from such a badge.

All of us are subjected to radiation exposure from a number of sources, both natural and artificial. This is usually referred to as **background radiation**. In addition, as we have seen, patients may be exposed to a radiation dose as part of diagnosis or treatment.

Radiation dose

As ionising radiation travels through tissue, it causes the formation of ion pairs. Ion pairs tend to occur in clusters in a very small volume (about $1\,\text{mm}^3$) and so, at the subcellular level, the amount of energy deposited is very large. This explains the extreme sensitivity of biological tissues to ionising radiation: the amount of energy which would raise the body temperature by 0.003 K if supplied as heat is sufficient to cause death if in the form of gamma radiation.

The measurement of radiation dose is a complex process. It begins with the physical measurement of the amount of energy deposited per unit mass of tissue, which is known as the **absorbed dose**. The unit of absorbed dose is the gray (symbol Gy) which is defined as the absorption of one joule per kilogram. Typical examples of this unit are shown in *table 7.1*.

Absorbed dose can be measured readily, but the biological effects differ for different types of radiation. Radiation which causes dense ionisation, such as alpha particles and neutrons, is termed high linear energy transfer (LET) radiation and is much more damaging than X- or gamma radiation. The problem of differing effects is overcome by the introduction of a **quality factor** which is used to weight the absorbed dose. This gives a quantity known as the **dose equivalent**, whose unit is the sievert (symbol Sv). Thus

$$\text{dose equivalent (Sv)} = \text{absorbed dose (Gy)} \times \text{quality factor}$$

For X- and gamma radiation, the quality factor is 1 and so the dose equivalent is numerically equal to absorbed dose.

The risk of illness and death from radiation depends also on which of the body organs are irradiated; some are more sensitive than others. So that the effects of irradiating different organs can be compared, the concept of **organ weighting factors** (W_t) has been developed. These have been defined by the International Commission on Radiological Protection and, at present, have the values shown in *table 7.2*.

A quantity called the *effective dose equivalent* (ede) is then defined as:

$$\text{ede (Sv)} = \Sigma\,(\text{organ dose equivalent} \times W_t)$$

Radiation	*Absorbed dose/Gy*
chest X-ray	0.0015
skin dose from a CT scan	0.05
gamma rays which would just produce reddening of the skin	3.0
absorbed dose which if given to the whole body in a short period would be fatal in half the cases	5.0
typical total absorbed dose to tumour in radiotherapy treatment lasting 6 weeks	60
absorbed dose to thyroid to treat thyrotoxicosis with iodine-131	65

● *Table 7.1*

Organ	W_t
gonads lung	0.2
red bone marrow stomach colon	0.12
thyroid liver oesophagus breast bladder remainder	0.05
skin bone surfaces	0.01

● *Table 7.2*

Source		*Effective dose equivalent*/µSv
natural		
radon		800
terrestrial gamma rays		400
internal radionuclides		370
cosmic rays		300
	subtotal	1870
artificial		
medical exposure		250
miscellaneous (flight, coal-ash, TV, etc.)		11
nuclear fallout		10
occupational exposure		9
nuclear power industry waste		2
	subtotal	282
	Total	**2152**

● *Table 7.4*

where the summation is over all organs which are irradiated.

The cdc can then be used to predict the risk of fatal cancer, which is presently defined as 5% per sievert. This means that, if 100 people were exposed to a dose equivalent of 1 Sv to the whole body, five of them would develop a fatal cancer.

Up to 100 mSv, no definite health effects have been found and no early deaths have been reported. Up to 10 Sv, radiation sickness, vomiting, skin burns and some increase in cancer results. At a total body dose of 100 Sv, the effects can be fatal, but this amount can be given in a radiation dose directed at a tumour.

For the special category of persons working with ionising radiation, the maximum permissible radiation dose to the whole body is 50 mSv per year. The maximum dose allowed to any individual organ is 500 mSv per year, with the exception of the eye, for which the limit is 150 mSv per year. For a member of the public, the whole body figure is 5 mSv and the individual organ limit is 50 mSv. It should be noted that medical exposure is excluded from this figure. In view of recent recalculations of the risk estimate, it is likely that the whole body exposure limit for people working with radiation will be reduced to 20 mSv per year while that for a member of the public will be 1 mSv.

Investigation	*Effective dose equivalent*/mSv
chest X-ray	0.1
spine X-ray	2.0
stomach X-ray	4.0
CT scan	1–3.5
bone scan	2.0
renogram	2.0

● *Table 7.3*

Calculations of the radiation dose for some medical examinations are given in *table 7.3*.

Background radiation

In the UK background radiation averages some 2.2 mSv per year. The major natural components arise from radon gas (originating from the radioactive decay of radium in rocks – particularly granite), cosmic and terrestrial gamma rays and from the naturally occurring radionuclides in our bodies (principally potassium-40 and carbon-14). By far the largest artificial component is due to medical exposure. Approximate annual values are given in *table 7.4*.

To put this in perspective 1 mSv is:

- the annual dose to the most exposed individuals from the nuclear industry;
- half the annual dose from natural radiation in the UK;

- 100 times the dose that would be absorbed by flying to Spain in a jet.

The total amount of background radiation is 2152 μSv which is just over 2 mSv. Since 1870 μSv is due to natural radiation there is little that we can do about it. The amount of radiation from medical uses is expected to decrease since techniques such as MRI involve no radiation.

The risk of dying through radiation can be compared with other risks. A man aged 40 has a one in 500 chance of dying of natural causes during a year. *Table 7.5* shows the risk of dying from various causes.

While the risk is very small, it is not zero. It is the aim of physicists to reduce the risk by using less radiation or other methods such as MRI which do not involve radiation.

Personal radiation monitoring

There are several different methods by which radiation can be detected but in health physics only a few particular types are useful. This is because many of the detectors must be portable and therefore of small size, and because of the information that is required about the radiation.

Film badges

Film badge dosimeters are worn by the great majority of people where work includes the use of ionising radiations. They provide a relatively cheap and easy method of detecting and measuring the radiations to which these people are exposed over a period of time. The badge is usually worn for a period of 1 to 4 weeks after which it is processed. The film is about 3 × 5 cm and is contained in a plastic holder which can be pinned to the person's clothing.

smoking 10 cigarettes a day	one in 200
road accident	one in 5 000
accident at work	one in 20 000
medical radiotherapy	one in 250 000

● ***Table 7.5***

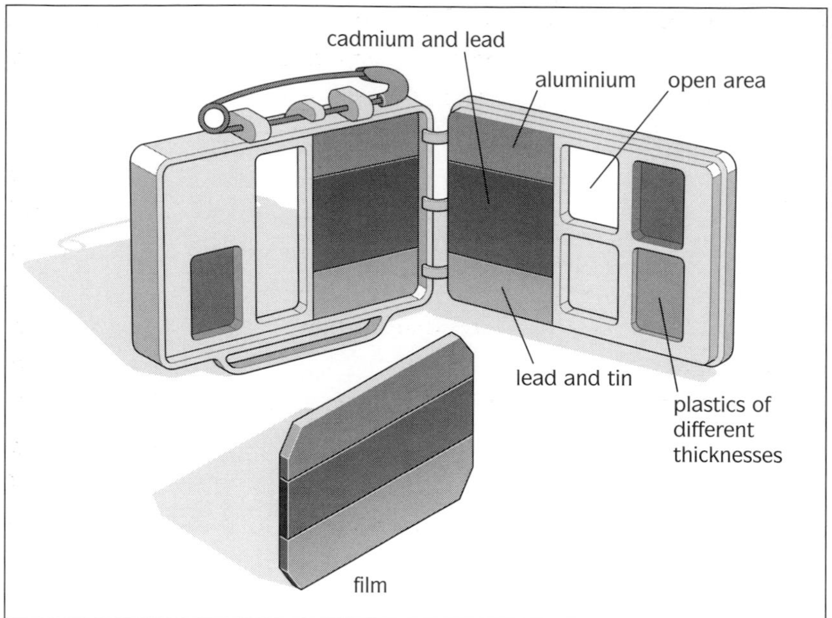

● ***Figure 7.1*** Film badge dosimeter.

A typical badge is shown in *figure 7.1*. One piece of film is used to detect the different radiations to which the person might have been exposed. This is achieved by covering the different areas of the film with a series of different materials which act as filters. One area has no filters so that it can measure the total dose. The film under the plastic windows absorbs differing proportions of different energies of beta particles, depending on the thickness of the plastic. When compared to the unshielded film, both the amount and energy of the radiation incident on the film can be estimated.

The metal windows absorb beta particles but can be used to differentiate between neutrons, and high and low energies of gamma and X-rays:

- the aluminium will absorb low voltage X-rays;
- the lead will absorb all but the very highest energies of radiations;
- the cadmium and tin will interact with neutrons to produce gamma radiation.

The amount of blackening in each area depends on the type and energy of the radiation to which the badge has been exposed. It can be accurately measured using a densitometer. The film is double sided with a fast emulsion on one side to detect small amounts of radiation, underneath which is a slow emulsion that allows the higher amounts of radiation to be measured. During processing the fast emulsion is measured first, then stripped away so that the slow emulsion can be measured.

The fast emulsion will absorb and measure radiation doses from 50 μSv to about 50 mSv. The slow emulsion will measure up to 10 Sv. The indium panel can measure doses higher than 10 mSv of thermal neutrons.

The advantages of film badge dosimeters are that:

- they are cheap;
- they give a permanent record of the radiation exposure;
- they are easy to use.

The disadvantages are that:

- the accuracy of measurement is only between 10 and 20%;
- the film is affected by temperature and humidity;
- the record of radiation is only known some time after the exposure has occurred.

SAQ 7.1

Film badges and most X-ray detection systems work on the same principle.

a Describe the key points of this principle.

b What is the disadvantage of monitoring radiation dose by this method?

Thermoluminescent detectors

The scintillation detectors mentioned in chapter 4 (page 40) emit light within fractions of a second of the ionising event. However, lithium fluoride takes a considerable time to return to the ground state and so can store information about an accumulated radiation dose, rather like a film badge. So it has become widely used as a radiation monitoring device.

Either a powder or a 'chip' of material is used. In order to read out the stored radiation dose, the material is heated to 250 °C, which causes the emission of light, the amount being proportional to the radiation dose to which the dosimeter has been exposed. This is measured by a photomultiplier as described for solid scintillators. The dosimeter is calibrated against known amounts of radiation so that the dose of radiation received by the dosimeter can be calculated.

The material is sealed in a thin plastic capsule which can be carried on the person to measure a personal dose, or placed on a laboratory wall to measure the radiation dose in a room over a period of time. There is no permanent record of dose (the reading can be obtained only once), but the device can be reused a large number of times. It is more accurate than the film badge and has a sensitivity which varies little with energy. Since it can record a dose of up to 1 kGy (compared to 1 Gy for the film badge) it can also be used to measure patient doses during radiotherapy.

SAQ 7.2

Compare and contrast film badges with thermoluminescent detectors.

SUMMARY

- A film badge is an inexpensive method of recording both the type of radiation and the dose to which the wearer has been exposed. The different types of radiation can be detected by the use of different absorbers in front of the film and the dose by the degree of blackening of the film. While the method is relatively easy, it is not precise and the detection takes place some time after the radiation has been absorbed.

Answers to self-assessment questions

Chapter 1

1.1
$$\text{Efficiency} = \frac{\text{power output}}{\text{actual metabolic rate} - \text{BMR}}$$
$$\frac{25}{100} = \frac{60}{\text{actual metabolic rate} - 60}$$
actual metabolic rate = 300 W

1.2 **a**
$$\text{Power} = \frac{\text{energy}}{\text{time}}$$
$$= \frac{500 \times 5}{3}$$
$$= 833\,\text{W}$$

b At $1\,\text{W kg}^{-1}$, BMR = 50 W
metabolic rate = 3382 W.

c Energy used in 3 s = 10146 J
$$\text{Volume of oxygen used} = \frac{10.1}{21.4}$$
$$= 0.47\,\text{dm}^3.$$

1.3 **a** $3.65 \times 10^6\,\text{J}$

b 1010 J

c This is greater than the power required to operate a 1 kW electric fire, which is $1000\,\text{J s}^{-1}$.

1.4 **a** Radiation, conduction, convection, evaporation and respiration

b Conduction and convection

c Put on some extra clothes.

Chapter 2

2.1 **a** The cornea is the outer part of the eye and provides the main refraction of the light. The lens is an active element which provides the fine adjustments.

b There is a large change in refractive properties without the face mask. With the mask, the refractive index of the air trapped in the mask make the refraction similar to that experienced above the water.

2.2
$$\text{Power} = \frac{1}{\text{focal length in metres}}$$
$$= \frac{1}{-0.25}$$
$$= -4\,\text{D}$$

2.3 Using the lens formula
$$\frac{1}{v} + \frac{1}{u} = \frac{1}{f}$$
$$\frac{1}{0.02} + \frac{1}{\infty} = 50\,\text{D}$$
This is the power required to focus at infinity. The power of the lens to focus at 1.0 m is given as
$$\frac{1}{0.02} + \frac{1}{1.0} = 51\,\text{D}$$
The power of the spectacle lens required is -1 D.

2.4 **a** At the near point the power of the lens is 50.5 D.

To bring the near point to have a distance of 0.25 m needs a power of 54 D. This means a spectacle lens of 3.5 D is required.

b If the accommodation is 3 D, the combined power at the far point is 51 D. The far point is at a distance of 1.0 m.

2.5 **a** Since the object changes shape with angle, the spectacle lens must have a cylindrical correction. This is used to correct the uneven curvature of the cornea in astigmatism.

b Since a person will see lines going more clearly in one direction than an another, then the power of the lens will be greater in one direction than in the perpendicular direction.

2.6 Red and green are the colours and difficulties may occur with wiring or signals. Electricians and train drivers may experience difficulties if there are problems with colour defects.

2.7 The use of leading edges and light give an effect of space and the use of subdued colours such as the stonework will give an effect of rest. Where colours such as red and gold are used, it will be for the parts of the building on which attention has to be focused.

2.8 A fresh, light atmosphere could be created by using green or blue, with some white to reduce saturation. A warm, sumptuous feel could be created by using red or purple, with very little white for some saturation.

2.9 For travel/business products, bold hues with a little white are used to emphasise confidence. Complementary colours are used. For leisure products, harmonious colours, with white for saturation are used.

Chapter 3

3.1 The pressures on either side of the eardrum are unequal. It can be reduced by rapid swallowing or by eating a sweet, which opens the Eustachian tube and equalises the pressure in the middle ear.

3.2
$$\text{Intensity} = 10 \log \frac{10^{-4}}{10^{-8}}$$
$$= 40\,\text{dB}$$

3.3 Test the patient's response to sounds both in air and applied to bone. In conductive deafness, in which the outer and/or middle ear is affected, the tests will show that air conduction is abnormal and bone conduction normal. If the problem lies in the inner ear, both will be abnormal.

Chapter 4

4.1 They will show up as almost the same density in an image, that is there will be little contrast between them and so little detail will be seen.

4.2 Cases where contrast between tissues is clear using X-rays, such as broken bones and teeth. Also where contrast materials can be used to show detail, such as barium for the stomach and intestines and iodine for blood flow.

4.3 A CT scan allows three-dimensional images to be recorded and displayed. Detail of organs deep in the body can be seen more clearly.

4.4 **a** It has a short half-life and emits only gamma rays which can be detected outside the body of the patient so it is useful in diagnosis.

b The generator can produce amounts of technetium-99m over a number of days, from which a number of patient doses can be prepared.

4.5 **a** A scintillation device contains a scintillator which interacts with radiation to emit light which can be detected and measured.

b A smaller number of larger holes increases the sensitivity but the amount of detail will be reduced.

Chapter 5

5.1 The ratio is 0.0009 which indicates that most ultrasound is transmitted and not reflected at the interface. So little difference will be seen between them and so little detail.

5.2 At the power levels used, ultrasound will not damage the fetus but X-rays can damage various organs.

5.3 **a** Doppler effect is used to measure the frequency shift as the reflecting interface moves.

b It can be used to measure the blood flow rate in, for example, a heart to check its functioning.

5.4 The right kidney is functioning normally, since the activity against time graph increases in the first few minutes and then decreases. The left kidney shows a continuing increase in radiation, indicating that no radioactivity (and so no urine) is being passed on to the bladder.

5.5 There is no radiation and therefore no danger to the patient. MRI also produces better contrast in images of soft tissues.

5.6 An LED produces light of only one wavelength which allows the absorption to be measured more accurately.

5.7 **a** An endoscope avoids the need for an operation or permits the use of a very small incision. There is also no heat produced at the end of the fibre.

b In total internal reflection the light hits the surface of the glass at an angle greater than the critical angle. So the light is reflected back into the fibre and does not escape through the surface of the glass. This happens because of the refractive indices of the glass fibres. Coherent fibres allow an image to be passed up the bundle while the incoherent bundle (which is cheaper) is used to transmit light down the endoscope to illuminate the viewing area.

Chapter 6

6.1 This allows the distribution of radiation in the body to be modelled in order to check that only tumour tissues will be destroyed. Isodose curves are lines joining points of equal percentage dose.

6.2 The accuracy of the beam, particularly at the edges, is better with a linear accelerator than with a cobalt source. This makes it possible to be more accurate about targetting cancerous tissue.

6.3 The source may not be placed accurately or may move inside the body.

6.4 The light is of a single wavelength and the power density is high.

6.5 **a** Neodymium YAG and carbon dioxide

b
$$\text{Power} = \frac{\text{work done}}{\text{time taken}}$$

$$\text{So time} = \frac{150}{20} = 7.5\,\text{s}$$

Chapter 7

7.1 **a** Radiation is absorbed by a photographic film which will blacken. The degree of blackening varies with the amount of radiation.

b The disadvantage is that the amount of radiation cannot be measured until a reasonable time has elapsed.

7.2 Thermoluminescent devices are more accurate (and can record lower doses) but may be more expensive than the simple film badges. The badge is, however, a single-use device, whereas the TLD can be reused a number of times.

Index (Numbers in italics refer to figures.)

A scan, 47, *48*
absorbed dose, 66
accommodation, 13–14
  change with age, 14, 17–18
acoustic impedance, 46–7
acoustic matching, 26
activity, metabolic rate for, 2
aerobic combustion, 1, *5*
'after loading' implant radiotherapy, 60
age, and accommodation, 14, 17–18
air gap in ultrasound scanning, 47
alignment, nuclear, *52*
alpha emission, 60
anaerobic combustion, 1, *5*
aqueous humour, 10
astigmatism, 16–17, 18
  contact lenses for, 19
  corneal reprofiling treatment, 64
atomic number, and attentuation, 35, 36
ATP (adenosine triphosphate), 1
attenuation coefficient, 35, *36*
audiogram, 30–1
auditory canal, *25*, 26
auditory cortex, *25*
auditory (Eustachian) tube, *25*, 26, 27

B scan, 47–8
back projection, 38
background radiation, 67–8
balance control, 27
barium, contrast agent, 37, 44
basilar membrane, 27, *28*
beta emission, 60
bifocal glasses, 18
birthmark removal, 62
blanket, reflective, 8
blind spot, *10*, 11
blinking, 10
blood, oxygen saturation measurement, 54–5
blood clot vaporisation, 62
blood flow monitoring, 49, 50
blood vessel dilation, for heat loss, 6
BMR (basal metabolic rate), 1–2
  increased during heat loss, 7
  body mass, 3–4
  temperature, 3–4
bone imaging
  MRI, 53
  X-ray, 36, 37
brain
  brightness perception, 19–20
  MRI, *54*
  role in hearing, 25
brain tumour
  detection, 45
  treatment plan, *58*
bremsstrahlung radiation, 35
brightness, 20; *see also* intensity

cancer
  destruction by laser endoscope, 62
  prediction, using ede, 67
  and relaxation times (MRI), 53
  see also tumour
cardiac studies, colour Doppler imaging, 50
CAT (computed tomography), 38, 45
cataract, 14, 62
cells, radiation sensitivity, 57, 66
ciliary muscles, 10
  accommodation, 13
  focusing, 11
cobalt-60, 59
cochlea, *25*, 27
collimator
  external beam therapy, 58, *59*
  in gamma camera, 41, 42
  in rectilinear scanner, 41
colour, and mood, 22
colour blindness, 21–2
colour Doppler imaging, 50
colour perception, social implications, 22–3
colour sensitivity, cones, 20–1
colour triangle, *21*
colour vision, 11, 20–1
  anomalous, 21–2
colour wheel, *22*
combustion, 1
compensators, 57, 58
complementary colours, 21, 22
Compton scattering, 35–6, 37
computed tomography (CAT), 38, 45
concave (diverging) lens, 12, 15
conductive deafness, 30, 32
cones, 11
  differential colour sensitivity, 20–1
  light intensity perception, 19
contact lenses, 18–19
contrast agents, radiographic, 37, 44
convection, heat loss by, 6, 7
convex (converging) lens, 12, 15–16
cooling: *see* heat loss; temperature
cornea, 10
  reprofiling, 63–4
Corti, organ of, 28
cosmic rays, 67
crystal, piezoelectric, 45
CT scanner, 38, 45
cycling, efficiency of, 5
cylindrical lens, 16, *17*

dB(A), 30
deafness, 30–2
death, risks/causes, 68
decibel, 29
  weighted scale, 30
depth of field, 12–13
diabetic retinopathy, 62, *63*
dioptre, 12
diverging lens, 12, 15
Doppler imaging, colour, 50
Doppler shift, 49, 50
Doppler ultrasonography, 49–50
dose distribution, X-ray treatment, *57*
dose equivalent, 66
dosimeter, film badge, 68–9

ear
  inner, 25, 26–7
  middle, 25, 27–8
  outer, 25, 26
  structure, 25–8
ear drum (tympanic membrane), *25*, 26
echo detection, ultrasound, 46
effective dose equivalent (ede), 66–7

electrons, secondary, 40
elution, in technetium generator, 39
embolism, static diagnostic study, 51
endolymph, 27, *28*
endoscope, 55–6, 62
energy
  and frequency, 34
  from food, 1, 2
energy production efficiency, 3
energy requirement, for activity, 2–3
environment, and heat loss, 7
Eustachian (auditory) tube, *25*, 26, 27
evaporation, 6, 7
excimer laser, 63–4
external beam therapy, 58–9
eye, compared with camera, 10
eye defects
  astigmatism, 16–17, 18
  hypermetropia, 15–16, 18
  laser correction, 62–4
  myopia, 14–15, 18
  presbyopia, 17–18
eye strain, 14

fetal scanning, 48, *49*
film, characteristic curve, *37*
film badges, 68–9
focal point, 12
focusing, of eye, 11
food, energy content, 2
food-to-energy conversion efficiency, 3
fovea, *10*, 11
fractionation technique, 57
frequency, and energy, 34
frequency range of hearing, 28, *30*
frequency response, hearing aid, 32
frequency shift, Doppler, 49

gamma camera, 41–2, 50–1
  image quality, 42
gamma emission
  from radionuclide, 39
  detection by scintillator, 40
  as X-ray substitute, 59
German measles, 31
glasses: *see* lenses
glaucoma, 11
gray (G), 66

hair cells, auditory, 25, 27–8
harmony, and colour selection, 22
head injury scanning, 45
haemoglobin, oxygen saturation measurement, 54–5
hearing, 25, 28, 30
hearing aid, 32
hearing defects, 30–2
heat loss
  compensatory reactions, 7–8
  detailed, 6–7
  and the environment, 7
  prevention, 8
  and size, 4
  see also temperature
hibernation, 3
horse power, 5
hue, 20
hydrogen concentration, MRI detection, 52, 53
hypermetropia (long sight), 15–16, 18
  corneal reprofiling, 63, *64*
hyperthermia, 6
hypothalamus, heat regulation, 6, 7
  cold-related failure, 8
hypothermia, 6

image intensifier, 37
implant radiotherapy, 59–60
incus (anvil), *25*, 26
insulation, preventing heat loss, 8
intensifier, X-ray, 37
intensity level, 28–30
intensity perception, relative, 19–20
intensity/intensity level relationship, 28–30
iodine
  contrast agent, 37, 44
  radioactive, 61
iris, 10
isodose curves, 57–8

kidney function study, by renogram, 51
kidney stone destruction, 61

lactic acid, 1
Lamour frequency, 52
laser
  in endoscope, 56, 62
  power characteristics, 61
  therapeutic uses, 61–4
lead wedge, isodose modification, 57, 58
lens (eye), 10
  power, 12, 13
  shape change, 13
  thickness determination, 47
lens formula, 14
lens-retina distance, 14
lenses (glasses)
  bifocal, 18
  contact, 18–19
  prescription, *17*
  types of, 12
LET (linear energy transfer) radiation, 66
light, diagnostic uses, 54–6
light intensity perception, 19–20
light-sensitive cells, eye, 11
lithium fluoride, 69
lithotripter, 61
long sight: *see* hypermetropia
loud noise, protection against, 26–7
loudness, and intensity level, 30
loudness detection, 28
lung scan, 51

magnetic resonance imaging (MRI), 51–3
  diagnostic procedure, 53–4
malignancy: *see* cancer; tumour
malleus (hammer), *25*, 26
mass, and BMR, 3–4
metabolic rate, 2
  basal, 1–2, 3–4
metabolism, 1
molybdenum-99m, 39
mood, and colour, 22
MRI: *see* magnetic resonance imaging
muscle healing, accelerated, 61
muscle power, 4–6
myopia (short sight), 14–15, 18
  corneal reprofiling, 63, *64*

near point, 14
noise, and deafness, 30
noise levels, 29

nuclear magnetism, 51–2
nuclear medicine, 39

old sight, 17–18
optic nerve, *10*, 11
optical fibres, endoscope, 55–6
organ of Corti, 28
organ weighting factors, 66, *67*
ossicles, *25*, 26
oval window, *25*, 27
oximetry, 54–5
oxygen, energy equlivalent, 2
oxygen consumption
  and BMR, 2
  and power output, 6
oxygen saturation measurement, blood, 54–5

pair production, 36
patient dose monitoring, radiotherapy, 69
perilymph, 27, 28
phon, 30
photochemotherapy, 64
photoelectric effect, 35, 36, *37*
  in radiography, 44
photomultiplier
  gamma camera, 41
  scintillator, 40
photon energy, for X-rays, 36
photopic vision, 19
piezoelectric effect, 45
pinna, *25*, 26
positron creation, 36
power, 4–6
power density, laser, 61
power of lens, 12, 13
precession, 52
pregnancy, fetal scans, 48, *49*
presbyopia (old sight), 17–18
primary colours, 21
prism, for eye defects, 17
psoriasis, photochemotherapy, 64
pulse echo detection, 46
pulse oximetry, 54–5
pupil, *10*

quality factor, radiation, 66

radiation
  background, 67–8
  cell sensistivity, 57, 66
  heat loss by, 6, 7
radiation dose, 66–7
  maximum, 67
  medical, 68
radiation intensity, and absorption, 35
radiation monitoring, personal, 68–9
radio frequency (RF) signals, in MRI, 52
radiography, 44–5
radionuclide, 39
radionuclide therapy, 59, 60–1
radiopharmaceuticals, 39
radiotherapy
  implant/surface, 59–60
  patient dose monitoring, 69
radon gas, 67
real-time scanning, ultrasound, 48
rectilinear scanner, 41
relaxation time, 52
renogram, 51
resolution
  pulsed Doppler ultrasonography, 50
  ultrasound scan, 47
resonance
  auditory canal, 26
  nuclear, 52
respiration, heat loss by, 7
retina, 11
  detached, 62
retina-lens distance, 14
retinopathy, 62, *63*
rhodopsin (visual purple), 19
rods, 11, 19
round window, *25*, 27
rubella, and deafness, 31

saturation (colour), 20
  emotional reaction to, 22
scalpel, laser as, 62
scanning, ultrasound real-time, 48
scintillation detector, 40
  personal, 69
scotopic vision, 19
sector scanner, 48
semicircular canals, *25*, 27
sensorineural deafness, 30, 32
shivering, 7
short sight: *see* myopia
sievert (Sv), 66, 67–8
simulator, for X-ray treatment, 58
single photon emission computed tomography (SPECT), 42
size, and heat loss, 4
sodium iodide
  gamma camera, 41
  rectilinear scanner, 41
  scintillator, 40
soft tissue contrast, MRI, 53
sound, 25, 46
sound detection mechanism, 28
SPECT (single photon emission computed tomography), 42
spin, nuclear, 51–2
stapes (stirrup), *25*, 26
subtraction techniques, radiography, 44–5
surface area, and BMR, 3, 4
surface radiotherapy, 59–60
sweating, 6
swept gain, 47

target volume, 57
targetting, radionuclide therapy, 61
tattoo removal, 62
technetium-99m, 39, *50*
tectorial membrane, 27–8
temperature
  and BMR, 3–4
  and size, 4
temperature regulation, 6–7
thermoluminescent detectors, 69
threshold of feeling, 29–30
threshold of hearing, 28, 29, *30*
threshold of pain, 30
thyrotoxicosis treatment, 60–1
transducer, piezoelectric, 45
tumour
  detection, CT, 45
  external beam therapy, 58–9
  volume determination, 57
  X-ray treatment, 57–8
  see also cancer
tympanic membrane (ear drum), *25*, 26

ultrasonography, 49–50
ultrasound, 45–7
  medical uses, 47–8
  resolution, 47
ultrasound therapy, 61
UVA (ultraviolet) light therapy, 64

vestible (inner ear), 27
visual acuity, 17
visual purple (rhodopsin), 19
vitreous humour, *10*, 11
volume, and energy production, 3, 4

water content, and relaxation time, 52–3
wavelength, differential sensitivity, 21
wedge, isodose modification, 57, 58
weight, and colour, 23
wind chill, 8

X-ray
  absorption, 35–7
  detection, 37
  diagnostic, 34
  gamma ray substitute, 59
  production, 34–5
  therapeutic, 34
X-ray film, 37
X-ray treatment, 57–8
  external beam therapy, 58–9
  implant/surface, 59–60
  planning, 57–8
  radionuclide therapy, 60–1
  simulator, 58
X-ray tube, composite output spectrum, 35

yellow spot, *10*, 11